Sticky Sales and Marketing

Produce Positive Long-Term Results and Relationships

Peter Lyle DeHaan, PhD

Book 2 in the Sticky series

ISBN:

979-8-88809-000-8 (e-book)
979-8-88809-001-5 (paperback)
979-8-88809-002-2 (hardcover)

Library of Congress Control Number: 9798888090015

Published by Rock Rooster Books, Grand Rapids, Michigan

Credits:

Copy editor: Robyn Mulder
Cover design: Taryn Nergaard
Author photo: Jordan Leigh Photography

To all who pursue sales and marketing in its various forms

Contents

SALES AND MARKETING

Promote a Product, Service, or Idea to Achieve a Desired Outcome

Every business or organization has a sales and marketing function. It's only the details that vary. They may have an existing department, or two, to address this need. Or the sales and marketing functions may fall under the purview of an individual, manager, or department. Regardless of whether it's structured or ad hoc, every group has a promotional element integral to it.

Some businesses sell a tangible product. It's something that customers can see and touch. It displays nicely on brochures and in ads. Buyers can hold it in their hands or try it. It's real.

Other businesses sell a service. A service is intangible. Buyers can't perceive it with their five senses. They realize benefits only after using the service. To sell service requires painting a picture of what life will be like once they've used the service. This is a harder sell because there's a delay between making the purchase and realizing the desired outcome. Amid this uncertainty, it's easy for the hesitant buyer to say no.

Some organizations—especially nonprofits—sell ideas. They promote concepts. Often their promotion efforts revolve around asking for donations. They use these contributions to cover overhead, fuel more sales and marketing initiatives, and address the needs of their target audience. They may even use a form of sales and marketing to find and reach out to their clientele, the population they seek to serve.

Beyond businesses and nonprofits, however, individuals must also use these tactics throughout their life. Whether it's finding a job, promoting a cause, or successfully interacting with family and friends, each interaction has some degree of sales and marketing—even if we don't call it that.

We must be able to successfully promote ourselves (sales and marketing) to land a job. The same applies if we're advocating for a cause or pitching an idea. And many interactions with family and friends involve a degree of negotiation—from "Pick up your room," to "I think we should buy this car," to "Which restaurant do you want to go to?"

If we don't fairly present our perspective, we lessen the chance of realizing the outcome we want or find acceptable. At the root of this idea of influencing others to achieve a desired outcome is sales and marketing.

That's why this book is important. Everyone's involved in sales and marketing to one degree or another. It's just that most people who don't carry a sales-and-marketing related title don't realize this truth.

Whatever your position or situation, it's important to master effective sales and marketing. This book will get you started. It will be up to you to apply these principles.

PART 1

Sales Management

I spent several years working in a multi-location call center that specialized in telephone answering services. As I moved into upper management and later became part owner, I took on the responsibility of sales management, along with my other duties.

Later I started a publishing company specializing in print and online periodicals. Once again, I found myself in a sales management situation, overseeing my media rep. She was not an employee, however, but an outside, independent salesperson. It was a different type of management experience for me, one I repeated later when I hired a virtual assistant to handle book sales.

THE SALES AND MARKETING SUCCESS FORMULA

Sales Success Comes through Attitude and Execution

People often ask, "How can I get more sales?" Increasing sales stands as a primary concern at most businesses. No one has ever told me their company closes all the deals they want.

I wish they would ask me easier questions: "How can I improve quality?" "How can I increase revenue?" "How can I reduce turnover?" I've dealt with all these issues, but the sales dilemma is trickier.

Sales managers seek a quick fix, a simple strategy. It's as if they expect me to say, "Invest X dollars in Y process to produce Z sales."

But there is no magic solution. If there were, I'd start a sales and marketing business. My clients would merely tell me their sales goals for the month, and I would fill their order. But it's not that simple. Selling is complex.

Though there are many sales strategies and marketing channels to pick from, they don't count for nearly as much as implementation. Implementation matters most.

Here then is my ultimate sales and marketing success formula:

Sales and Marketing Success =
Personnel + Attitude +
Execution + Management

Personnel

Sales staff is the first element in the success formula. Without the right people in place, nothing else matters. This starts with finding the ideal person for the job. Over the years, I've hired many salespeople.

What is true for all job candidates is even more valid for sales applicants: you see them at their absolute best during the interview. In fact, even mediocre salespeople know they must give their best sales performance during the interview. If they can't sell themselves to you, how can they ever sell your product or service to someone else? To cut through all of this, I have a few key questions I like to ask sales candidates:

How much did you make at your last job? If they made six figures, but can only earn half that at your company, they're unlikely to work out. They'll be unhappy with their lower compensation, develop a negative attitude, and leave as soon as a better-paying job comes along.

Conversely, if they barely cracked the poverty level at their last position, they may be out of their league to produce at the level you expect. Ideally, their target compensation working for you should be 5 to 25 percent higher than what they made at their past job.

How much would you like to make at this job? The response to this is most telling. Why? Because if it's unreasonably high, they won't be satisfied working for you. On the other hand, if it's lower than what you are prepared to pay, then they'll coast once they hit their target compensation.

Look for a salary expectation that's consistent with what you can deliver but will still motivate them.

Would you like to work straight commission? I don't advocate that *anyone* earn a straight commission. However, I pose this question to throw them off track and gauge their response.

To make this work, don't ask the question directly but back into it. If they're at all good with sales, they will have already regaled you with their accomplishments, assured you that they'll be your best salesperson ever, and pledged to produce at a level beyond your wildest expectations.

And, if they have moxie, they may even say you'd be foolish not to hire them or they may suggest your company will fail without them. (Yes, I've heard this from sales applicants.) Given all of this, they assert that you must pay them top dollar.

At this point, I lean forward and whisper, "I don't normally offer this, but based on your track record and past performance, I think you're worthy of special consideration. I suggest we consider a compensation plan where you'll be highly rewarded for your results and given an open-ended opportunity to exceed your compensation goals."

Then I pause before I ask, "How would you like to work for straight commission?"

First, watch if they can smoothly react to an unexpected question. Next, see how they retreat from their prior boasting. Often a more realistic picture emerges. Last, their counterproposal will reveal what they expect for base pay and how much they're willing to put on the line in the form of commissions, incentives, and bonuses.

If this offer offends them, simply apologize and say that, based on what they said, you thought this idea would appeal to them.

Never once did I have a boastful sales candidate want to work for straight commission.

Attitude

Having the right sales staff, however, is just the beginning of the success formula. They also need to have the right attitude. How many times have you seen salespeople talk themselves into a bad month? The thinking goes like this: "Last year this month was bad. Is it always bad? I better brace myself for a bad month." It becomes a self-fulfilling prophecy, and then they have a bad month.

Another self-defeating attitude is negativity. Consider, for example, the salesperson who says, "Direct mail? That won't work!" And with that attitude, it never will. Or how about, "That didn't work last time, and it's not going to work now!"

Are they willing to try new things? If they're open to innovative ideas, then they have a much greater chance of success than if they're closed-minded.

Strangely, all too many salespeople would rather continue to do what has failed in the past than try something new.

Execution

Linked to attitude in our success formula is the proper execution. In fact, without the right attitude, successful execution is impossible. I've seen ideal marketing plans flop because of poor execution. Conversely, I've seen the most ill-conceived strategies succeed brilliantly because the sales team diligently, steadfastly, and consistently implemented them.

Quite simply, there needs to be a plan. Then meticulously follow the plan. And hold those involved accountable for their work. This brings up the fourth element: management.

Management

The glue that holds the success formula together is management. Good management starts with hiring the right salespeople, giving them excellent training, providing them with proper compensation, and motivating them to produce.

Follow this with a sound marketing plan and a supportive environment in which to implement it. Finally, sales management means an ongoing time investment to encourage, observe, teach, and adjust what your sales staff does.

Succinctly put, management keeps them on task and holds them accountable.

Seldom is a salesperson successful without ongoing managerial attention. They need encouragement when they are down and applause when they make a sale. Keep them responsible for their schedule and liable for their results. This takes considerable time and effort. As such, proper sales management is not just one more hat to wear, but a full-time job.

Successfully managing salespeople is challenging work. It takes time, perseverance, and dedication. But then, don't all things that are worthwhile?

Sales Management Success Tip

Find the weak link in your company's success formula. Then implement a plan to fix it.

Commission Plan Failure

Ill-Conceived Incentive Programs Can Actually Hurt Sales

John was a salesperson who periodically visited our business. His company supplied specialized equipment to our industry, and we regularly bought from him. He cultivated relationships with many people in the company, including me, even though at the time I was scarcely an influencer—let alone a decision-maker. Yet John paid attention to me, and I looked forward to his visits and the cordial friendship we shared.

John once told me that his company provided a decent base pay along with a commission. The base pay was enough to live on, but to go beyond that the commission was essential. When my company made a significant purchase from John, I assumed he would be ecstatic.

He was not. He was quite nonchalant about his significant sale.

"Won't you get a nice commission?" I asked him in private.

He shook his head.

I gave him a quizzical look.

"I only get a commission if my sales exceed last year's. And last year was a banner year for me, three times what I've ever sold in one year. I was the top salesman of the company and ranked high on the all-time list.

"I won't be able to match that this year, not even close. That means no commissions."

I considered what John said. "Does that mean you need to try to alternate between good years and bad years so you can at least earn a commission every other year?"

John again shook his head. "Last year's sales number is my target going forward to earn any commission. And since my base pay is fixed, if I want to earn more, I'll need to change jobs."

John continued his affable interaction with our business, but he seemed to have lost his enthusiasm. His company's commission plan had disincentivized their top salesman, serving to push him away.

Much later in my career, the company owner presented me with an intriguing incentive plan of my own.

Though it wasn't sales related, he intended it to motivate me to produce even greater results.

As he explained the criteria to calculate my bonus—which could double my already nice base pay—I planned what I'd do to maximize my bonus.

My eagerness didn't last long, however, when he got to the last provision of the plan, a caveat. It said that the payout was contingent on company profits. That meant I could meet every objective and receive no bonus if the company had a bad year.

He never asked me what I thought about the plan.

If he had, I'd have told him that to work all year for a bonus but then not receive it would be the biggest demotivating factor I could face. As far as my long-term employment with the company was concerned, it would be in my best interest to *not* pursue the bonus, even though that's how I was wired.

I ignored the goals of the incentive plan and continued to do what I thought was in the best interest of the business. Even so, by year end I did earn a couple thousand dollars bonus. But I didn't care. I didn't get my hopes up because I knew that each year was contingent on the company's profitability.

My indifference toward the bonus surely perplexed my boss, but he never asked why the plan failed to motivate me.

My employer no doubt put that last provision in place because of a negative experience that another company owner had encountered. She had put her operations manager on an incentive plan that rewarded her for growth, effectively for sales and customer retention. The manager responded with diligence to the incentive and the company grew under her direction. She earned nice annual bonuses.

A few years in, the owner realized the operations manager would make more than she would—much more. The owner paid the agreed upon amount and dropped the plan. The operations manager soon left.

Sales Management Success Tip

The purpose of a commission or bonus is to motivate salespeople. Evaluate your plan from their perspective to ensure that it does, in fact, incentivize them. Make sure there are no provisions that would cause them to not do their best or that might provoke them to leave.

An Unconventional Hiring Approach

Desperate Times Call for Desperate Measures

H er words surprised me.

"I can't run this ad!"

The rep's response caught me off guard, but it wasn't completely unexpected either. "I agree that it's a bit unorthodox."

"I might get fired if I publish this." She fumbled for words. "Or we might get sued."

"It's just a classified help wanted ad," I said. "What are your concerns?"

"Well . . . to start with, I doubt it complies with EOE requirements. And then there's truth in advertising too."

"I worked hard to write an ad that is both legal and ethical. I feel I've done that and see no reason the ad can't run."

She paused and let out a deep sigh. "Let me check with legal."

I doubted their small operation had a legal department or even legal counsel, but it sounded better than her saying she was going to check with her boss. Though I'm sure that's just what she did.

She agreed to call me back with the decision.

I waited.

As I did, I contemplated what plan B would be. Yet this *was* plan B, and there was no plan C. I only resorted to my unconventional ad because I was desperate to hire someone to handle our sales.

The office in question was in a resort town. We served area businesses and needed a salesperson if we were to grow and realize the market's potential.

Currently, the operations manager was handling sales in addition to her other duties, but she already had too much to do. Responding to a sales inquiry was one more distraction from her primary role. And if she closed the sale that meant even more work for her and her team.

She had no incentive to handle sales inquiries and even less interest in closing a sale.

That's why I needed to hire someone for sales. I'd been trying the usual approaches for months and had come up empty. That's when I stumbled onto plan B.

Waitstaff and Salespeople

My idea was to target restaurant waiters. Here's why a waiter would make a good salesperson.

First, a successful waiter knows how to interact with a wide range of people with different temperaments and expectations. They know who they can banter with, who wants to establish a rapport, and who wishes to keep a professional distance. The same skills are critical for sales.

Second, a successful waiter knows how to read people. Waiters not only listen to what the customers say, but they also tune into the tone of voice and are careful observers of body language. They've honed all three aspects of effective communication: words, tone, and nonverbal. They excel in each area. Sales staff must do the same.

Third, successful waiters receive generous tips. The expectation of a financial payoff from each patron motivates them to do whatever they can to maximize their tip. The same principle applies to sales. Commissioned salespeople want to maximize their commissions. Though waitstaff receive tips and salespeople receive commissions, both have a financial incentive to do their job with excellence.

But why would a successful waiter want to exit the restaurant industry to work for a 9-to-5 business? There are several good reasons.

The Benefits

The first reason is better hours. Restaurants schedule staff to work when people want to eat. This seldom fits working eight-hour shifts. It requires short shifts, long shifts, split shifts, and even double shifts.

The second benefit is a more consistent schedule. The work schedule for most restaurant employees varies from one week to the next. There's a constant juggling of shifts and trading hours. This is ideal for a person who likes variety and is okay with their plans being flexible. Some people can build their life around an ever-changing work schedule, but few people can do so for the long-term.

Third is full-time employment. The nature of restaurants, with most of their activity happening around mealtimes, not only makes an eight hour shift unlikely, but it also requires a lot of part-time staff. But most people want full-time work—because they want full-time pay.

Fourth is protecting evenings and weekends. Though it's not absolute, many restaurants—especially the upscale ones—do most of their work in the evenings and on weekends. Again, this is ideal for some people but not for most—and not for the long-term.

Working in business sales is a full-time, daytime, weekday job. It smartly addresses the downsides of working at a restaurant.

The Ad

A few days later, my ad contact called me back. "I can't believe it," she said, "but they approved your ad!"

It ran that weekend and for the next seven days. I waited for the calls to roll in. Five people answered the ad. Though I'd hoped for more, five responses were more than the none I had been getting.

Of the five, three were interested, two scheduled interviews, and one showed up.

Brandon, however, was not who I envisioned. He fell short of expectations. Yet he responded to my ad for exactly the reasons I theorized. He was tired of the restaurant schedule and wanted full-time, business-hours work.

He was the best candidate I interviewed, but he was also the worst. I hired him anyway. This wasn't because he was a great match for the position but because I was desperate to hire someone.

The Results

We went through a few days of training, and I turned Brandon loose to work on his own. Brandon, I soon learned, needed on-site supervision, but I was seldom on site. For a while I checked in with him daily by phone, and he told me what I wanted to hear (his waiter skills coming through). But I doubted his veracity.

His results disappointed me as well, with his sales numbers only slightly surpassing the results of the office manager.

Because I was desperate, I worked with him to improve his sales, but the outcome didn't change. He quit before I could fire him.

The Mismatch

I think my logic in targeting waiters was sound. The failure was that it didn't apply to our company's situation. We needed an employee who was self-motivated and needed minimal daily accountability. Had I been running a retail operation, with on-site management and day-to-day oversight, I suspect Brandon would have excelled.

Sales Management Success Tip

Never hire someone because you're desperate. Better to be short-staffed than stuck with the wrong salesperson.

[In case you're wondering what the ad said, I'm sorry to say that I don't remember. But I can assure you it was a wonderful one.]

EARNING EXPECTATIONS

Sales Compensation Requires Careful Consideration

O ur company had multiple offices. Those in larger cities called for having full-time salespeople. At one of those offices, one with a larger geographic work-force to draw from, my ads always received a response. Yet not all respondents were good fits.

For one applicant, Jennifer, our in-person interview was going quite well. She currently worked in retail sales and wanted to move her sales skills into the business-to-business environment. Professionally attired, she conducted herself well, having an engaging personality and a suitable level of enthusiasm—coming across as neither desperate nor aloof.

The 24-Hour Rule

As our interview wound down, I wanted to hire her. Though I had never offered an applicant a job at the end of the first interview, I expected I would eventually do so. As a rule, I always make myself wait at least twenty-four hours to process my interaction with the applicant more fully to make sure I hadn't overlooked something.

One time, however, I came close to breaking that rule, but fortunately I did not. Because the applicant came from out of town for her interview, I asked my operations manager to take part in the interview process. The applicant enthralled me but not my operations manager. Her apprehension over the candidate gave me a needed pause.

Fortunately, I resisted the urge to offer the woman a position on the spot. Instead, I told her I'd be in touch. In the hours after the interview, I considered her conduct. I realized I'd focused on her many good points and brushed aside the multiple red flags that went with them.

The next day it was clear she wasn't a good match for our company. Hiring her was bound to produce conflict throughout her employment. She would be a high-maintenance salesperson. And, despite her confidence to the contrary, I doubted she could produce the sales results she promised.

I wisely decided to pass. This experience confirmed the importance of waiting at least a day before offering a salesperson a job.

How Much Do You Want to Make?

I had one last question to ask Jennifer before we wrapped up our interview. I asked, "How much do you want to make in this position?"

She had her answer ready and flashed a confident smile. Her response, however, shocked me.

Even though I had told her this was a salaried position with commission, she gave her answer in terms of an hourly rate. This revealed a disconnect between the entry-level job mentality of where she was at and the professional sales opportunity she applied for. Her perspective of hourly pay was misaligned with my salaried compensation paradigms.

More telling, however, was the low number she gave me. It was about twice minimum wage. Though I hadn't given our salary range, what I planned to offer far exceeded that amount.

I knew she would be completely satisfied to earn our base pay. As a result, she'd have little incentive to work hard to close sales and earn a commission. This is because she'd already be making more than she wanted to.

Though I could've offered her a much lower salary—one slightly less than the amount she wanted to make—and thereby motivated her to sell, it wouldn't be fair. And I wouldn't feel right about it.

I wrapped up the interview and thanked her for her time.

Too Much

Though Jennifer disqualified herself by having low expectations, I've more often experienced the opposite extreme. These people cruised through their interviews but then ruled themselves out with their lofty compensation goals.

By design, I expected a successful salesperson to earn commissions equal to 35 to 50 percent of their base pay. In doing so, they could earn a good living.

Though they could surpass that amount and earn higher commissions, it seldom occurred—and never on a regular basis. No one ever earned a sales bonus that approached their base pay. It was the nature of what we sold, the amount of a typical sale, and the number of hours in a workweek.

One cocky applicant insisted upon a nice six-figure base pay. He claimed he was worth it. Regardless of if he was, I knew from experience that he'd never come close to making enough sales to justify such a lofty salary. It simply wasn't achievable. Even if he accepted my offer of a much lower base, he wouldn't stick around and would leave as soon as a better opportunity came along.

For him, I smiled and segued into my 100-per-cent-commission ploy. He backpedaled quickly. His overconfident demeanor disappeared, yet he held fast to his need for a high base salary.

Another slick-talking interviewee waved off my offer of commission. "I don't need an incentive to motivate me. I'll be more successful than anyone you've ever hired." Of course, he wanted an astronomical salary as well. Our ensuing discussion about why I wasn't open to his request became quite terse. The interview didn't last much longer.

These are examples of why I always guard against sales candidates who try to convince me to do something I don't normally do or doesn't feel realistic.

Just as Jennifer set her sights too low and didn't get the job, these two applicants—along with others like them—missed out because their expectations were unrealistically high for our industry.

Sales Management Success Tip

Never offer a sales applicant a job on their first interview. Always give yourself time to fully process how well they align with your company and goals.

And never allow an applicant to *sell* you on the need to offer them a compensation plan that's unrealistic for your organization.

Not All Sales Experience Applies

Successful Selling in One Area Does Not Universally Apply to All Others

F rank had a successful sales career in one industry, but his desired career path wasn't an option at that company. To pursue his dream, he needed to change employers. He soon landed a job as a sales manager, the next step in his career path.

Frank looked to apply the selling paradigms he learned—and successfully applied—at his prior job to his charges at his new job. When he told me his plan, I was skeptical. It struck me as impractical and unworkable at his new company—even though it had served him well in his prior sales position.

The strategy was simple. End one day by setting appointments for the next day. Since the contacts occurred over the phone, the goal was one appointment per hour, resulting in eight appointments each day. This provided eight opportunities to close a sale every workday. Then, after the final appointment of the day, begin setting appointments for the next.

Since he didn't ask my opinion, I didn't give him one—even though I really wanted to.

As I understand it, his sales team wasn't impressed when he presented his grand idea. They gave him a half-hearted assent and made some effort to set appointments, but no one came close to the goal of eight per day.

After a month of him trying to hold them accountable, he abandoned his strategy. Notably, there was no overall measurable sales increase for the month, one person even sold less, and none of them were happy.

Not All Strategies Transfer

At Frank's prior job he sold manufactured products to an identifiable niche market. Each existing customer in his territory would make ongoing purchases throughout the year. And each prospect in his territory needed what he sold. The question was whether they would buy from him or his competitors. Most ended up choosing him.

To meet with his customer base, he would visit them in their offices. Because of travel time, he could only set two or three appointments a day. It was easy for him to do because these meetings were with people who wanted to talk with him. In many cases they already knew what they would order when he showed up.

His goal was to build a rapport with each customer, supply the information they wanted, and offer strategic advice as needed. Then he would take their orders. Frank was professional, personable, and reliable. This allowed him to achieve success and earn a nice income.

Frank's new company, however, didn't sell a product. They sold a service. And each sale was a one-off; there were no chances to make repeat sales. Though there were occasional opportunities for later upsells, the more likely scenario was a customer scaling back to save money.

Setting appointments in this industry was also a challenge. Prospects were entrepreneurs or small business owners. They were busy, often out of the office, and hard to reach by phone. They'd call when it worked best for their schedule. That meant sales staff functioned primarily in a reactive mode. Prospects would call, and the salespeople would react. If they weren't available when the call came, they might not get a second chance. For them, availability was the key to success.

Frank soon realized his sales training, experience, and success didn't transfer to his new employer's industry. He needed to revamp his strategy to better align with what his company sold and how its prospects functioned.

Key Differences to Consider

Product versus Service: Selling a product is different than selling a service. A product is tangible; a service is not.

A customer can look at a picture of a product or hold it in their hands. With their senses they can assess its functionality. A prospect can't look at a picture of a service or touch it. They can only imagine how it might function and if it'll produce the desired outcomes.

It's much easier to sell a product than a service. Success in the first area does not guarantee success in the other.

Repeat Sales versus One-Time Purchases: Making a new sale to an existing customer is much easier than making a first-time close. Repeat customers understand the product's utility and know your company. They've already made the buying decision once, so making a later purchase is an easy decision.

Successful salespeople are often effective because they can make recurring sales to existing customers. It's much harder to find success when each sale is to a new prospect.

High-Ticket Items versus Low-Cost Purchases: The price of the product or service has two ramifications.

The first is the amount of commission. Ten percent of a hundred-thousand-dollar sale is much more significant than ten percent of a ten-dollar sale.

The second is the amount of work needed to make the sale. High-cost items may need several people at the prospect's organization to sign off on the purchase or multiple rounds of approval. It may mean adding the cost to next year's budget, which will delay the purchase for a year or more. Inexpensive items or services are open to spontaneous purchase and easier to sell.

Differentiated versus Commodity: If your product or service is different from what your competition offers, even unique, prospects who need it will eventually buy from you. All that's needed is patience—which is a good reminder to never write off a prospect who doesn't buy right away.

A commodity product or service, however, is available from multiple providers. This includes you and your competition—all of them. Prospects can buy from you, or they can buy from somebody else. It may come down to price, availability, or how well you connect with the prospect.

Sales Management Success Tip

Recognize that sales skills that worked well in one job or industry may not readily transfer to another. Therefore, build on what you know to create an approach that fits each situation.

EXPERIENCE VERSUS EDUCATION

Evaluate If Recent College Grads Are Right for Your Company

When hiring a salesperson, you can seek someone with relevant experience or someone with related education. Sometimes a candidate has both. The opposite is when they have neither.

I'd been hiring salespeople who had varying degrees of selling experience, though sometimes it was minimal—as was the case when hiring Brandon, the waiter. Not satisfied with the results, I opted for a different approach. I targeted college graduates who had an interest in sales and some relevant education, even if tangential.

The Marketing Major

Jessica was about to graduate from college with a degree in marketing. She applied for a sales job with us as her last semester of college wound down. I offered her the position, starting when she graduated. She was excited, and so was I.

Before long I welcomed her to our company and began her training. This involved educating her about our business, the services we offered, and our typical customers. She took it in with great enthusiasm. Before long she felt ready to begin work, and I turned her loose.

Since we worked in different offices, I checked in with her daily by phone and weekly in person. When her enthusiasm ebbed, I offered encouragement. She received it well and resolutely pushed forward. She made a couple of sales and was on track to become a successful salesperson for our company.

Imagine my surprise when, in her second month of employment, she resigned. She decided she didn't like sales after all and felt customer service was a better fit. She'd already found that position with a different company.

Disappointed for myself, I was also disappointed for her. She had spent four years in college pursuing a marketing degree with an expectation to go into sales. Yet within two months of graduating, she abandoned her career in sales and switched tracks to pursue customer service, a career independent of her marketing degree.

The Liberal Arts Graduate

Lauren arrived soon after Jessica. She had recently graduated from a well-respected, highly ranked liberal arts college. In addition to being professional and intelligent, she carried herself well, was articulate, and had an engaging personality. Not to diminish others I'd interviewed or our existing staff, but Lauren was a step above them. She was that good.

Interestingly, she worked part-time at a high scale restaurant, the kind where one table could generate a $100 tip or more. Her weekly tips roughly equated to the base pay I was prepared to offer her. As I gently probed into her motivation, I learned that she wanted full-time, business-hours work in a professional environment. She wanted to move beyond part-time, evening and weekend restaurant work.

I was excited to have someone of her caliber on our team, offered her a position, and she accepted. She started right away. Training went well and quickly. Soon she was working on her own and closing sales. As with Jessica, I checked in with her daily by phone and weekly in person. Since the two worked in different offices, I introduced them to each other so they could encourage and support one another. But at about that time, Jessica left.

A few months into her employment with us, Lauren also realized a disconnect. All her college classes had stressed collaboration, group exercises, and working in teams. They did this because that's what employers said they needed.

Yet her role with our company required her to work independently. Though other people worked in her same office, they weren't in sales. And I was off-site.

In short, she wasn't part of a group. She wasn't on a team, something four years of education had trained her for. She tried to adapt to working independently—and by my assessment had done so successfully—but it wasn't an environment she wanted to remain in. She needed regular interaction with others. With reluctance, she gave me her two weeks' notice.

Training and Support Is Key

These aren't cautionary tales to avoid hiring recent college grads. Instead, it's a call to evaluate your company's management and training of salespeople. With the proper infrastructure in place, many companies strategically target recent grads and successfully bring them into their company.

There are several reasons why this is a good approach.

One is that since they're new in the workforce (at least as a full-time employee in a professional environment) they have no negative habits for you to counteract or retraining to do. You start fresh. As a bonus, they're used to learning.

Another is that they're more apt to have youthful enthusiasm for their work. Also, since this is their first *real* job, they want to succeed. And, although a healthy work-life balance is important to them, they also have certain lifestyle expectations they want to meet. Having a job with open-ended sales potential can do just that for them.

The key to making this work is having a well-honed onboarding process and management structure in place to supply daily support, encouragement, and oversight.

I did not have that to offer Jessica and Lauren. I wasn't a sales manager. Instead, sales management was one more task I tried to squeeze into an already too-busy workload. And it wasn't a priority for me. Other aspects of my job held more interest. Sales got whatever I had left. Sometimes that was enough; sometimes it wasn't.

Also, since we seldom hired salespeople—averaging about one per year—we had no structured training program in place. It was more of an ad hoc approach. This worked for some people, and it didn't work for others.

Sales Management Success Tip

Examine the sales management and onboarding structure you have in place. Then target applicants that align with it. Alternately, restructure your training and support processes to better match the applicants you receive.

A Day of Sales Calls

Interact with Sales Staff in the Field to Determine Their Strengths and Weaknesses

Mitchell came to us in need of a second chance. With a lifetime of experience in the business world and history of sales success he seemed overqualified to work for our company. But he assured me this was the right job for him at this point in his life. I agreed and offered him the position.

It was a newly created role in a large but underdeveloped market for us where we had a presence but little market share. The metropolis offered much potential, and Mitchell relished the opportunity as well as the challenge. He breezed through training. I set him up in an office, and he went to work.

He quickly filled his sales funnel with promising prospects, and we were both excited. But he struggled to close them. On each weekly phone call, he'd regale me with the potential that sat in his sales funnel, especially his most promising prospect. Should he close the sale, it would be our biggest client to date.

We both expected it to happen, but after a couple months of futility, he was perplexed, and I was frustrated. I needed to see him in action if I hoped to figure out what was going wrong.

I blocked out a day on my calendar and told him to schedule appointments with his three most promising prospects: one in the morning and two in the afternoon.

The Meeting Objective

On the appointed day, I drove to his office, picked him up, and we headed to his first appointment. It was the big prospect he'd been courting for months. Before we went in, I asked him what his objective was for the meeting. He didn't understand my question.

I explained that each interaction with a prospect must have a goal to move them forward in the sales process. This could include providing them with more information, learning how soon they wanted to move forward, or asking for the sale.

He wasn't sure.

I suggested we try to find out how quickly they wanted to act and see if we could get them to commit to a date when they wanted this to occur. He concurred.

I told him to take the lead. He agreed.

He introduced me to her and began making small talk. She seemed irritated. After letting him flounder for a few minutes, I eased myself into the conversation.

"In an ideal situation," I probed, "when would you like to see a transition to our service occur?"

Her outlook brightened a bit, and we launched into a meaningful discussion about her business, a strategy to move her account to us, and what outcomes she could expect.

Twenty minutes later Mitchell and I left her office with a signed contract and a check in hand.

Once back in my car, Mitchell looked at me and shook his head. "How did you do that?" I explained to him my *secret*—which I'll reveal to you later, in the first chapter in "Part 2: Sales Tips."

A Couple of Feds

As we drove to our second appointment (which was a business lunch at a local diner, something I hadn't expected or wanted), we discussed the objective of the meeting. This is when I learned that we weren't meeting with someone in his sales funnel, but with a new lead that had only come in yesterday. He hadn't done any work on it.

Knowing what my first question would be, however, he already had an answer for the goal of our meeting: it was to find out what they were looking for. This is something he should have done before setting the appointment. I explained that prequalifying a prospect was a smart idea before agreeing to meet with them, especially for lunch.

I wore a suit and Mitchell wore a sport coat and tie. This was the perfect attire for our first meeting, but apparently a bit overdressed for our second. The two men wore business casual. When we sat down in our booth, one glanced nervously between Mitchell and me. Then he blurted out, "You two look like a couple of feds." He shuddered a bit and forced a smile. I did too.

If he had experience with federal agents interviewing him and was uncomfortable because we reminded him of those interactions, I wondered what type of business he was in and if we wanted anything to do with him or his company.

Again, we had agreed that Mitchell would take the lead, and I would step in if I felt it was appropriate. The guys were tight-lipped about the type of business they were starting and talked in vague generalities that could apply to most any entrepreneurial endeavor. This made it hard for us to evaluate how we might be able to help them or even if we could.

Not meeting our goal, we finished our meal and paid the bill. Mitchell tried to follow up with them later, but they ghosted him. Given how uncomfortable I was with their demeanor, I wasn't disappointed.

A Cancellation

As we left the diner, I learned that our third appointment had cancelled the day before, and Mitchell had been unsuccessful at finding a replacement prospect to meet with. I was disappointed, feeling I hadn't used my time with Mitchell to its full advantage. I suspect he was just as discouraged.

Summary

We did earn a large sale that day, landing the biggest client our company had ever seen. Even though I closed the sale, I gave him credit for it, explaining that he had nurtured the prospect and prepared her to buy. Also, we had a 50 percent close rate for the day, another thing to relish. I tried to encourage him by focusing on the positives.

However, I also had doubts, wondering if Mitchell could be a successful sales rep for our company. Though he had the experience and the background, the results were decidedly lacking. I needed to figure out a way to help him turn things around—or we would need to part ways.

Sales Management Success Tip

Periodically go on sales calls with your sales team, especially those who underproduce. Demonstrate sales techniques to them by example. Use each situation as a teachable moment. Figure out what you can do to help them succeed.

Anything for a Sale

Closing a Sale but Alienating a New Customer in the Process Is Bad Business

Back when my family had an entertainment subscription (aka cable TV), a new network launched, and we wanted to watch its shows. I wondered if my provider would offer it, but repeated contacts to our provider via email resulted in no responses. Next, I called them, but they couldn't give me any answers.

During this time, a direct mail piece arrived from their competitor. It offered an attractive price, free installation, and new equipment, including a DVR (remember DVRs?). This appealed to me since our receiver and remote (free promotional incentives from our existing provider) were wearing out. The DVR would be a bonus.

Upon calling the prospective provider, I talked to a helpful and confident agent, Karl. My first question was if they carried the network. Karl knew all about it and assured me they did.

Upon further digging, however, I learned we wouldn't save money by switching. But changing providers would get us the new network and new equipment, including a DVR. I confirmed my understanding of what Karl said and placed my order.

A few days later, the installer arrived and set up the system. He gave a quick overview of its operation as he waited for the programming to download. I asked for the channel number of the new network. "I don't know offhand," he said, "but it's there someplace. If you can't find it, call this number." He handed me an information sheet, which included a phone number. Then he left.

Thirty minutes later, and frustrated, I dialed that number. "I'm sorry," the agent said. "I can only help you with installation issues, and this isn't an installation question. You'll need to call the provider." (Karl, it turns out, worked for an authorized agent and not the company.)

The provider's call center told me it would be an extra $5 a month to get the new network. Mad at this unexpected news, I called my buddy Karl. Unfortunately, he was no longer my buddy.

"I only deal with sales questions," he said. "I can't help you." Then he hung up.

My wife, who is tenacious in righting wrongs and fixing the unresolvable, took over our quest to watch the new network. Over the next few days, she called Karl, the service department, the installation line, and the billing department, as well as any other number she could find.

Several days and too many calls later, she resigned herself to accept that I'd been had.

During our dealings, we'd received many conflicting explanations:

- The network is part of your service package.

- The network is available for only a dollar more a month.

- The network is available for five dollars a month.

- The network is not part of your local channels (even though it was broadcast locally).

- The network is available everywhere but in your area.

There is much to learn from this saga. One miscommunication had widespread ramifications for us.

One person's words, either by intention or ignorance, resulted in more than a dozen follow-up phone calls and a new customer who is angry and feels maligned. It will take much effort to overcome such a bad start.

As such, several recommendations are in order:

Training

If the miscommunication was out of ignorance, then better sales training could have averted the whole ordeal. Unfortunately, the payback from training isn't directly quantifiable, while sales numbers are. This is a dilemma that sales managers must acknowledge and grapple with.

Call Monitoring

If the miscommunication was intentional, then some policing is in order. Active monitoring might have caught the error, could have uncovered the rogue employee, and certainly would have minimized all employees' willingness to lie to close a sale.

Incentives and Measurements

What gets measured gets done, and what gets paid for gets done better. Again, if the miscommunication was intentional, then it was a calculated lie to make a sale.

Unfortunately, sales departments' reward systems often serve to promote activity that's detrimental to an organization's overall best interests. Always keep the big picture in mind.

Third Party Accountability

Whenever a company hands off contact to an authorized agent, they need to hold the third party accountable. The parent company's reputation is at risk, and they need to confirm they're properly represented.

This involves more than just tracking monthly sales totals or the cost per sale.

Consistency

All staff must have the same information, supported by the same technology, and reinforced by training. This helps to ensure they'll give customers the right answer—every time.

Furthermore, they must synchronize this with their websites and coordinate it with marketing pieces. This supplies a singular answer for every employee, spread across multiple channels.

Quickly Salvage Mistakes

There's a ripple effect when a mistake happens. This occurs both within the company as more people are pulled into the problem, as well as outside the organization as others hear about the issue. Both take their toll.

Empower front-line employees to act and to solve pressing issues, not just be encouraged to end the call so they can take the next one.

Problem Resolution

After many calls, an agent finally apologized, but no one ever said, "What would you like done to resolve this?" No one ever suggested a course of action or recommended a solution.

We never did get the network we wanted from that provider, but Karl, who will say anything to close a deal, did chalk up a sale.

Sales Management Success Tip

Don't look at sales numbers in isolation. Instead. consider how sales and marketing initiatives fit into your company's overall long-term goals.

PART 2

Sales Tips

T hough much of my experience has revolved around managing salespeople, there have also been times when I was the salesperson. This occurred when I worked for a few years as a consultant. If I wanted to work, I needed to sell. This was an uneasy prospect for me, however. Since I was selling myself, it seemed boastful. I never found a comfortable balance in doing so.

Later I had a media rep to handle sales inquiries with my publishing business, but there were times when I also did sales. Toward the end, I sold more than she did. I also sold a new promotion plan to our advertisers for one magazine after she told me it wasn't possible. Most exciting, I turned our least profitable property into the one with the highest ROI.

Here are some of the tips I've learned through my sales experiences and in interacting with other companies over the years.

THE EITHER/OR CLOSE

Ask Your Prospect to Choose Between Two Options, Both of Which Meet Your Objective

Remember when I went on the sales call with Mitchell? In a few minutes I closed the sale he'd been working on for a couple of months. The "secret" sales technique I used is no secret at all. It's the simplest closing technique available and the easiest to master. That's why I use it.

It's called the either/or close.

The premise is simple: give your prospect two options and ask them to pick the one they like the best. It's easy for them because it's the simplest of decisions to make. There are only two possibilities with no variables: it's A or B.

The beauty of this approach is that either choice meets your overall aim of closing the sale.

Here's how this worked on the sales call Mitchell and I made: Once I established a rapport with the prospect,

I asked one simple question: "Would you like to start service this weekend or wait until next week?"

She paused for only a moment and said, "This weekend." At that point the sale was made. I only needed to finalize it by having her sign the agreement. She was eager to do so.

I told her we'd send her an invoice for the set-up fee and first month's payment. But she waved me off and had a check cut while we waited. That's how motivated she was in switching over to our business. And it all happened because I used the either/or close.

The either/or close is my default method of closing sales. I use it every time. And I close well over half of those sales.

Usually, my two options relate to starting dates. I've used this for both selling answering service and selling advertising. If they're willing to give me an answer, they've mentally already decided to go with my company, even if they don't yet realize it. The only time they vacillate and decline to pick one of the two options is if they're truly undecided, have a concern I haven't addressed, or aren't a serious buyer.

Another pair of options is picking between two rate plans. But I never ask them to pick between the two highest packages. Instead, I ask them to pick between the one I feel will work best for them and the one I feel will work second best. That way we both win. I get a sale, and they get a solution that will work well for them.

There's a variation of the either/or close that I call the special incentive close. We'll cover that in the next chapter.

Sales Success Tip

There's much we can learn about the sales process and selling techniques. Don't discount the advanced skills and learn whatever you can, but also embrace what is simple and works for you.

Use it as your go-to closing technique. For me it's the either/or close.

THE SPECIAL INCENTIVE

Capitalize on Naturally Occurring Motivators, but Don't Manufacture a False Sense of Urgency

In the last chapter I mentioned a variation of the either/or close. I call it the special incentive close. Here's how I use it when selling advertising for my publications. In essence it's buy now and receive a special incentive or buy later without it.

Sometimes an advertising prospect has selected the rate plan they want to be on, but they still haven't fully committed. Though they've mentally agreed by selecting which package they want, they're delaying in signing the paperwork. That's when I give them a nudge with a variation of the either/or close. It's a special incentive.

Receive Bonus Coverage

"The next issue goes out in three weeks," I say. "If you sign up today, you'll get all the online benefits right away, but I won't start your billing until the issue goes out. You'll get three weeks free. Shall we do that?"

This is usually enough to nudge most prospects forward to sign the paperwork. Remember, they've already mentally committed when they picked which advertising package they wanted. The special incentive close merely gets them to formalize what they've already agreed to in their mind.

Lock In Today's Rate

A variation of this happens toward the end of the year when I consider rate increases for the upcoming twelve months. Though I don't like to use this tactic often, because it strikes me as a little too close to being sleazy, I do tap it for people I can't move from mental acquiescence to actual commitment. And, of course, it only works in the fall.

I simply tell them, "We're looking at possible rate increases for next year, but if you sign up before the next issue goes out, you can lock in this year's rate for all of next year." This usually gets them to move forward.

If they press me for what the increase might be, I either give them a realistic range (for example, 3 to 6 percent) or I'll share last year's increase.

Sometimes I already know what the new rates will be. Then I give them actual numbers. "Next year, this advertising package is going up 8 percent, but if you sign up before year's end, you can lock in this year's rate for all of next year. That's a savings of . . ."

Avoid a False Sense of Urgency

I've seen salespeople, however, who overuse this sales tactic. They do this by manufacturing a disingenuous reason to buy now. This is clearly a sleazy ploy, and ethical salespeople should avoid it.

It might be that they offer a special deal for people who buy today, "so that I can meet my quota for the month. Can you help me out?" A variation of this is ". . . so that I can keep my job." They tug at our compassion, and we want to help them. Their maneuver often works.

Or: "My boss is gone today," he whispers, "so if you sign up now, I'll give you an extra bonus—just between us. What he doesn't know won't hurt him." The incentive could be a discount, free add-on service, or even a BOGO (buy one and get one for free). By lowering his voice, the salesperson treats it like it's a deep secret between you and him.

I experienced the most deplorable abuse of this tactic once when shopping for a used car. The owner of the lot gave me what I considered to be a fair price for the car I was interested in. But it was a one-day-only deal. When I told him I wanted to check out a couple other cars down the street first, he clarified his offer. It was only good until I left. If I came back—even an hour later—I'd have to pay full price.

I didn't think he'd hold to his threat, but he delivered it convincingly enough to cause me to doubt. In the end, I reluctantly bought the car from him. Though I don't feel he charged too much or sold me a lemon, I forever hold a bad impression of him. And he heightened my overall dislike for car salespeople.

Sales Success Tip

Offer prospects a special incentive whenever you can do so honestly and ethically. But avoid abusing this tactic by creating a false sense of urgency or lying to your prospect.

Three Lessons in Retail Sales That Everyone Needs to Hear

A Saga of Shoe Shopping

When my daughter was in college and on break, we'd often go for walks. Though I enjoyed our father-daughter time, I began to decline her requests. This wasn't due to a lack of interest but because blisters would result.

My daughter took the lead in finding a solution. "We're going to need to get you a new pair of shoes—good walking shoes."

She was right, but I groaned. I avoid shopping. If I can't buy it online or talk my wife into picking it up, I often go without.

"Where will we go?" I dreaded the answer.

"The mall."

That was precisely what I didn't want to hear. I gathered my courage, and we headed off.

She selected the best entrance, designed to minimize my exposure to the hostile mall environment. Guiding me to the escalator, we descended into the belly of the beast. She led me through a maze of turns and corridors, deftly emerging at the entrance of a large shoe store.

Disingenuous Service

Overwhelmed, I took a deep breath and stepped into its bright lights and imposing displays. I had an impulse to flee, but my shopping-savvy daughter guided me to the men's sneakers section in the back.

The two clerks both attended to other customers; we were on our own. As I tried on pair after pair, one concern permeated my thoughts: how would I know which choice would not cause blisters? I already owned two blister-inducing pairs and had no interest in a third. Eventually a clerk wandered over.

Looking past me, she addressed my daughter. "So, are ya still finding everything all right?" She said this in such a way that any response other than "Yes" would admit ineptitude.

Before I could ask for help in a way that didn't sound too pathetic, she retreated to the safety of the register counter. From that bastion, she and her coworker re-sumed what seemed an all-important conversation.

Realizing the likelihood of buying shoes from either of them was low, my daughter suggested we try another store.

No Service

A scant twenty seconds later we strode into the next shoe shop for another round of futility. Three staff members huddled around the register as though pro-tecting it from outsiders. Two uniformed clerks didn't even pause their animated conversation to acknowl-edge our arrival. The third, a smartly dressed twen-ty-something female, looked up, flashed a broad smile, and demanded, "Hi ya! How ya doing?"

I responded as positively as possible, only to realize she wasn't talking to me but my daughter. Apparently not hearing us, she repeated her greeting, this time, louder. We recoiled at her intensity and veered to the perimeter of the store. There were only displays—no stock—so without the help of staff, we had no choice but to leave.

Great Service

By now, I was more than ready to go home, but with no idea how to leave and find my car, I remained captive to the whims of my shopping buddy. Around the corner was a third shoe store. It was the smallest of the three and crowded. Even so, the manager greeted us with a genuine smile. For the first time I wasn't invisible.

Although the clerk made overly assertive recommendations and talked incessantly about all things footwear related, he at least helped us.

As soon as the goal of blister avoidance came up, he zeroed in on the problem. He offered an unexpected, yet convincing, explanation, along with a "guaranteed" solution. Within minutes, we left with a shoebox in hand and smiles on our faces. The return trek to the car wasn't as difficult as I imagined. Soon we were home, trying out my purchase.

Retail Reflections

Primarily configured for self-service, the first store offered only passing interaction. The second one offered no help and barely acknowledged our presence, yet its configuration made self-service impossible. No help meant no sale. The final shop gave useful input through staff that wanted to help.

The goal at all three companies was to sell shoes. Furthermore, they hired and paid employees to make that happen. And they trained their staff.

What was the difference? Quite simply, implementation.

A Parallel Scenario

I've seen these three situations played out many times. For the sake of illustration, let's imagine three operations that sell widgets over the phone.

I call the first company. An automated system answers. After endlessly pressing options without any result, I hear an option to talk to a real person. I press zero but nothing happens. After more frustration, I hang up.

I call the toll-free number of the second company. An enthusiastic rep abruptly answers, but she can't hear me. We may have a bad connection. Should I talk louder? More likely, however, is that the idle conversation of her coworkers is either too noisy or too interesting for her to hear me. Regardless, she repeats her greeting, this time louder. She pauses for a second and hangs up. Then she probably complains to her coworkers about stupid callers.

Discouraged, I call the third company. A person answers. He listens. Once he knows what I want, he offers assurance. "Let me help you find the right widget for your situation." He does—and I'm glad to place my order.

The goal of companies is to make money. Effective sales are the way to do this, with employees hired and trained for that goal. Don't let ineffective automation, poor supervision, or negative work environments get in the way, whether retailing shoes, hawking widgets, or selling your own products or services.

Sales Success Tip

Pretend you're a prospect at your company. Identify and correct the parts of your processes that drive customers away or thwart sales success.

A Shocking Experience

Customer Service Excellence Can Boost Sales

I received a subscription invoice for a magazine I had never heard of nor received. This didn't surprise me. This used to happen a lot. Magazines would show up and later an invoice arrived to continue my "subscription."

I scrawled "please cancel" on the invoice and returned it in their pre-paid envelope. That was the end of it, or so I thought.

A few days later, the magazine arrived. I looked at it and was interested. I read it. I enjoyed it and wished I hadn't canceled it. Maybe I *had* ordered the publication after all, though I couldn't remember doing so.

I pondered what to do. It wasn't fair that the publisher had sent me the magazine in good faith but wasn't going to collect their payment. I also wanted to receive future issues. Yet I wondered if I had the energy to contact the publisher and try to resolve it.

The Dreaded Call

Notice that I said, "try to resolve it." My overall experiences had so numbed my expectations that I doubted I'd succeed.

How many phone calls would I need to make? How many times would they transfer me to the wrong person or department? Would someone hang up on me? Might they tell me to call another number and then another, only for them to direct me back to the first? Could I understand and communicate with the agent? Would they understand the situation and know what to do? Might I make things worse?

These questions swirled in my mind. They were all based on frustrating experiences I'd had with other companies. I gathered my resolve. Dreading the task before me, I blocked out time to focus on this chore.

A Successful Outcome

Things got off to a good start when I found a prominent "subscription number" in the magazine. I took a deep breath, and I dialed their toll-free number.

An actual person answered.

The agent was both pleasant and professional. She seemed happy to talk to me. I could understand her—every word. I explained my dilemma, and she understood. No transfer, no pondering, no delays.

"I can take care of it," she said with confidence. And she did.

Summary

Resolving an issue on the first call isn't hard to do, but in my experience, it's rare.

It starts with intentionality. The essential elements are hiring qualified people, training them well, and empowering them to take proper actions.

Beyond these basics, provide clear instructions and develop flexible policies with a customer-first perspective. Wrap up by celebrating excellence and rewarding successful outcomes.

In place of dread, work to make sure your customers and prospects look forward to contacting you. In this way your customer service staff can best support your sales and marketing efforts.

Sales Success Tip

Make problem resolution frictionless for your staff and painless for your customers. Sales will result.

PUT THE CUSTOMER FIRST

Achieve Better Outcomes by Making the Prospect a Priority

I put off buying things. It's not because I procrastinate (at least not too much), don't like making decisions, or don't want to spend money. Sadly, the reason I often avoid buying what I want or need is simply because it's too much of a hassle. More to the point, going without some items is less inconvenient than investing the time and enduring the frustration to try to buy them.

Too many of my negative experiences relate to cell phones. It's a sad commentary on the industry. Fortunately, I've seen some positive correction in recent years. Nevertheless, the following experience from a couple decades ago still supplies us relevant insight.

For quite some time—okay, more than a year—I considered getting three more cell phones. I expected to sign up for a family plan, adding phones for my wife and our two kids. At a few bucks more each month per additional phone, it was a no-brainer. I could then find my wife when she was out, keep in touch with our daughter in college, and give a nice perk to our teenage son.

However, I put off moving forward because I so dreaded the process.

A Rigid Requirement

The time to act finally came. I gathered my courage to move forward. I called my existing carrier. They confirmed I'd met my contract requirements and could make changes.

"What I want," I explained, "is to get on your family plan and add a couple of phones." I was even willing to buy the other phones.

"No problem," the rep assured. "Each additional phone is only ten dollars a month and some phones are free if you sign a one-year contract . . . and," she added, "we can replace your current phone too."

This sounded too good to be true, but before I could tell her to go ahead, she interrupted my short-lived euphoria.

"Oh, there's a problem . . ." The problem was that they required me to be on a plan with more minutes—many more.

I tried every angle I could think of. More phones, fewer phones, buying the phones, longer contract, and not replacing my current phone.

She was intractable. "No, you still need to move to a bigger plan."

Doing so, and adding just one more phone, would more than double my rate. I'm not opposed to spending money, but I hate wasting it. Her solution didn't seem very *family* oriented. I told her so.

Then I tried an emotional gambit. "I guess I'll just need to cancel my service and go with another carrier."

"If you need to, go ahead, but you won't find a better deal." Her arrogance appalled me. "We've all got basically the same rates."

"Okay, let's leave everything as is for now," I said, not wanting to burn my bridges.

A Cavalier Attitude

Now it was time for plan B.

If only I could talk to someone face-to-face, to do business with a local person who would take a personal interest in helping me. I headed to the local store of a national carrier that does *lots* of TV advertising. Several aspects of their pitch appealed to me. I was confident they had a plan for me, and I intended to complete my mission in one stop.

I walked in the door and, as my eyes adjusted to the lighting, a stereotypical salesperson charged toward me—must be they were on commission. Brashly, he ushered me into his office and grilled me on what I wanted. With each request, he would nod and affirm he could do that. He was typing things into a computer and then he gave me a total. His solution was twice the amount of the family plan quoted by my current carrier. The rates weren't all the same after all.

I couldn't suppress my laugh. This irritated him.

"Okay," I said. "Now, let's get realistic."

"Nope, that's the best I can do," he answered.

Thinking we were still pursuing a mutually desired goal, I began to reply, when he stood up and gestured toward the door.

"Sorry I can't help you." He said the right words, but his tone conveyed the opposite. Maybe he wasn't on commission after all.

Not ready to give up, I asked if he had any literature about what we had discussed. "We don't have any." He sneered. "It's all online. Just go to our website and order your phones there."

In five short minutes, I went from ready-to-buy to unable to leave fast enough.

Online, I later discovered his company had a much more attractive package, closely matching what I wanted. I'd have bought it had he only offered it.

A Calculated Lie

On to plan C. Originally, I intended the phones as a surprise, but I needed help. I enlisted the aid of our daughter, who was home for the summer. Having just completed her summer-school job, she had extra time on her hands.

We listed the features we wanted. Then she got busy doing research online. The next day she presented me with a spreadsheet of comparisons. She explained what she learned, we talked about options, and she made a recommendation. It required a two-year contract, so I wanted to make sure it was right. We discussed each plan's weaknesses, the fine-print exceptions, and ways they might charge us for services we thought were free.

I agreed with her recommendation and we made a list of questions, the chief one being whether the plan's coverage area included the city she'd move to next year.

I called the carrier and verified our understanding of the details. He confirmed everything, and a sale was imminent.

Last, I asked if they covered the city in question. "Yes, we do." The rep said this a bit too quickly and with a false confidence. I doubted his answer and prodded some more. He kept to his answer, but I doubted his honesty.

I ended the call without placing an order. It was good that I didn't, as we later found a coverage map—albeit a bad one—online. The map showed the city in question annexed from the coverage area.

He lied to me—imagine that. I assume he knew the truth but reasoned that before I figured it out, he'd have made a sale and earned his commission, with no recourse on my end.

A Successful Outcome

My daughter and I discussed our remaining options and revisited the website of our fourth choice. Thinking I would once more attempt working with a local rep, I called their closest office. After several rings, a recording informed me that no one was available and disconnected me.

Next, I dialed their toll-free number. This rep was actually helpful. Why are accommodating employees such an anomaly?

She was the first truly pleasant and knowledgeable person I had talked to during this whole quest. She patiently answered my questions with professionalism. She confirmed the plan's coverage and told me about their 14-day, no-obligation trial.

I placed my order. The phones arrived the next day.

Sales Summary

With my existing carrier, I was willing to buy a second phone, pay an additional $10 a month, sign a long-term contract, and run the risk of overage charges. They were only willing to upsell me and lost a customer.

At the second carrier, their rep got greedy—or was undertrained. He ushered a ready-to-buy prospect out the door.

For the third carrier, a cavalier lie on a critical issue dropped them from further consideration.

After a bad start at the fourth carrier, a well-trained, professional, customer-focused phone rep made a nice recovery and closed a sale.

Sales Success Tip

Seek to help your prospect achieve their goal, and you're more likely to achieve yours.

THE OPTIMUM TIME TO SELL

If We Determine When Prospects Aren't Open to Buy, Our Experience Will Confirm It

T yler, it seemed, was content to earn his base pay. He showed little incentive to close sales or earn any commission. Because he had one job to do—sell accounts—I expected his close rate would far exceed the office manager's, who only handled sales when she had to, squeezing the task into her already too-busy day.

Yet Tyler merely matched her low sales numbers, if that. I expected him to close five times as much and hoped he would get ten. Instead, he merely maintained the status quo.

When I reiterated to him the goal of closing one sale every business day, instead of two or three a month, he was quick with his response about why that wasn't realistic.

"I can't close any sales on Monday because everyone is always too busy after the weekend. They're in recovery mode and don't want to talk."

I raised an eyebrow but that didn't dissuade him from continuing.

"Fridays are just as bad because prospects are focused on wrapping up their week. The last thing they want to do is talk to a salesperson. They're already thinking about their weekend plans."

"You just ruled out 40 percent of your work week." I made no attempt to hide my dismay.

He didn't take the hint to stop talking and plowed forward. "The first thing in the morning doesn't work, nor the end of the day. Before and after lunch is bad too. And, of course, lunch is out."

I shook my head, but he didn't notice, or it could be he didn't care.

"Wednesdays are bad too," he said. "I haven't figured out why yet. Maybe it's some sort of midweek slump." By now he was smiling at his great insights. I was not.

"So that leaves Tuesdays and Thursdays," I said, not trusting myself to say much more and remain civil.

"Yep," he said. "The ideal time to sell is on Tuesday and Thursday afternoons between 2 and 4:00 p.m." He gave an excited upward tip of his head, as if to confirm his great wisdom.

"I disagree with your logic," I said, "but even at that you have two opportunities to sell each week. That means you should have at least eight sales each month.

He shook his head. "Not every meeting will result in a sale."

This was the first thing he'd said that I agreed with, but I wasn't going to let him know. Instead, I pressed into his illogical assessment. "Today's Wednesday. Who did you talk with yesterday afternoon?"

He hung his head and mumbled, "No one."

"Who are you going to contact tomorrow afternoon?"

"I'm still working on that," he said.

A good sales manager would have fired him on the spot. I didn't. A few weeks later he saved me the trouble of doing so.

I've also had sales staff try this approach using a seasonal mindset. "August was bad last year," they say. "Are all Augusts bad? That must be why my sales are down." Sometimes they extend their logic to cover the whole summer, one fourth of the year.

Then they make similar excuses for any week that has a holiday in it, sometimes for the whole month. By that logic, they eliminate another 20 percent of the year.

Yes, sometimes it's more difficult to close sales, but that's no excuse not to try. If they think they'll fall short, they surely will.

What if they tried a different tactic in August? What if they encouraged each prospect to prepare for fall by buying now? This way they'd have the decision behind them when they returned to work after Labor Day weekend. What a smart way to move into fall.

Don't think about what you can't do. Think about what you can do.

Sales Success Tip

Your outlook determines your results. Don't talk yourself out of having a good sales day, week, or month. Instead, expect success throughout the year. Plan for it, and you'll be more apt to realize it.

CHECK YOUR EMAIL TO CLOSE MORE SALES

Don't Lose Leads from Inaction or Oversight

I once sent out an email to 156 salespeople to verify some information they had submitted to my company. This information was for a printed directory to connect potential buyers to them. There was no charge for the listing.

Several of those email messages bounced back immediately, with varying types of unresolvable error messages. Several more came back after four days of trying. To their credit, some people responded at once or the next day. After a week, I sent a follow-up email to those I hadn't heard from yet. A few more addresses were undeliverable on the second round.

With both mailings, I received many "out-of-office" messages. Few of them were the out-on-a-sales-call variety, but rather, they were the on-vacation-for-two-weeks type. This wouldn't be alarming, if not for the fact that I sent my message to email address-es specifically intended to receive sales inquiries.

The result was that of 156 original contacts, thirteen (8 percent) were bad email addresses and eighty (51 percent) were apparently good email addresses, but no one bothered to respond. Only sixty-three (40 percent) replied.

Remember, this was not a list that I bought or har-vested, but the result of self-submitted email addresses from people who wanted prospects to contact them. This was an astoundingly poor 40.4 percent response rate.

Can you imagine if a company was that apathet-ic about their telephone sales inquiries? The analogy would be that on 8 percent of attempts the caller would receive a "nonworking number" recording or a busy signal, 51 percent would ring but no one would ever an-swer, and only 40 percent would have a person answer and respond. With a record like that, how long would a company stay in business?

Before you criticize me for implying that email is comparable to the telephone, I must point out that email is the default communication channel for an in-creasing number of people who disregard phone calls.

And these people are becoming the decision makers at your prospects' offices.

If you want more sales for your company, the simple solution might be to check your email.

And here are some more tips to help ensure email sales success:ereHere

Start with Your Website

Check your website periodically to make sure it's working. Sites can go down (usually temporarily, sometimes permanently), pages can get deleted, links break, domain names become pointed to the wrong place—or to nowhere—and so on.

Then verify all the contact information listed on your site. Also test each contact option, such as contact forms and posted email addresses.

Keep Track of Your Email Addresses

Assign an email administrator to track all email addresses your company uses. This includes both the ones to individuals, as well as general-purpose ones (such as sales@, info@, webmaster@, and so forth).

When an employee leaves, don't just deactivate their email, but forward it to the email administrator who can respond or route messages to the proper person.

Test Your Email Addresses

Once you've accounted for all your email addresses, check them regularly to make sure they're working. This is especially true of department and company-wide addresses. Also, test every email address that has an auto-response message or is forwarded to another mailbox. Both situations are prime areas for problems to occur, and they can easily remain undetected for a long time.

The most critical email addresses are the published ones. This includes those listed on your website; printed in ads, directories, and listings; and posted online on other websites. Test them daily. This testing can be automated. Just make sure someone checks the logs to ensure the program is running and address any errors.

Develop a Vacation Policy

Establish a policy for staff email when they are on vacation. Short of having employees check their email while gone (an unwise requirement), an auto-response message is the minimal expectation. This message must provide the name, number, and email address of an alternate contact.

A preferred approach is to not inconvenience the client or prospect and simply have someone check the vacationing staff's email account for time-critical messages.

This is an excellent reason to keep business and personal email separate. Just as you don't want personal email encroaching on business hours, it's wise to keep business email from detracting from personal time.

Heighten the Importance of Email

With any mission-critical technology there are back-up options, contingency plans, notification procedures, and escalation steps. The same needs to occur with email.

Verify Your Staff

Until now, I've addressed the technical side of email. Don't discount the human aspect. Left unchecked, salespeople can become lackadaisical or delete any message that doesn't sound like an easy sale. The only remedy to correct this abuse is through monitoring and verification.

Sales Success Tip

Treat email as an essential sales tool and respond quickly to messages, regardless of whether it sounds sales-related or not.

PART 3

Marketing Management

Marketing drives sales. You can't hope to have the latter without the former. Over the years I've tapped many marketing channels. Some were successful and others not so much.

At the call center where we specialized in telephone answering service, I made extensive use of Yellow Pages ads. Remember them? It was a different time. Though the Yellow Pages books still exist in some markets, the internet rendered them obsolete. I also ran print media advertising in local business-oriented magazines. I even dabbled in radio and cable TV ads.

For my consulting business I relied on print media advertising and trade shows, but most of my work came through networking, with some word-of-mouth support.

My periodical sales also occurred through networking and trade shows. Yet the publications themselves became their own marketing tool and the best way to showcase their promotional impact. In recent years my marketing reach has been bolstered by SEO (search engine optimization) and the reputation of my long-standing websites with thousands of pages of valuable, industry-specific content.

Most recently I've focused my marketing attention on promoting books. My website is the center of that activity, strengthened by favorable SEO and content marketing posts—I started blogging in 2008. I connect with my fans through my weekly newsletter and enjoy good open rates and meaningful interaction. Social media plays a small but worthwhile role in pointing people to my website. This sets a great foundation for book sales, but I drive additional sales through internet marketing.

The channels you use will differ from mine, but most are worthy of consideration regardless of what business you're in. We can learn useful lessons from all of them.

Consider some of the common marketing channel options:

- Retail

- Direct mail

- Direct mail followed by a phone call

- Print media

- Brochures and sales literature

- Telephone (inbound and outbound telemarketing)

- Broadcast media (television and radio)

- Trade shows

- Books

- Networking

- Referrals

- Cold calls

- Websites

- Content marketing

- Social media

- Social media advertising

- Advertising platforms and banner ads

- Email and newsletters

Each of these marketing channels has a proven record of producing sales. Unfortunately, these same methods have also been total failures. Campaigns that consistently generate high sales numbers for one company have been colossal flops at others.

The distinguishing factor is not the strategy, but what surrounds it. Remember my ultimate sales and marketing success formula that I covered in the beginning of the book?

Sales and Marketing Success =
Personnel + Attitude +
Execution + Management

Keep this in mind as we move forward.

Marketing Options

Know Your Options to Craft an Informed Promotion Strategy

We've never had more marketing options available to us than we do now. It's an exciting time to be a marketer. It's also a confusing time. There are so many options it's easy to become overwhelmed.

Each channel provides an opportunity to promote yourself, your products, or your services. We'll divide these into traditional marketing and newer online marketing options.

Traditional Marketing

Traditional marketing options include retail, direct mail, print media, the telephone, broadcast media, and even books.

Retail: Perhaps the oldest marketing option is retail, dating back thousands of years to a farmer or craftsman selling their wares in the town's marketplace. Physical retail outlets still exist today, though they now face pressure from online retailers.

The goal in retail is simple. Get the prospect into your store and make the sale. Other forms of marketing feed the retail channel to draw people to the store, be it physical or online.

Direct mail: For as long as we've had the opportunity to send content to others via mail, we've been able to use it for marketing. In its most basic form, direct mail can blanket a geographic area.

More sophisticated direct mail efforts target people by demographic or socio-economic data. And specific mail communication can go to existing customers and prospects.

Print media: The marketing channel of print media includes magazines and newspapers. Though neither has the reach and impact they once had as a marketing tool, we shouldn't overlook them. This is especially true with magazines, where niche productions that target specific subcategories have replaced general-purpose publications.

For any industry or interest group, there's assuredly a publication that addresses them. Though most of these are online, some still print and mail their content. Many consumers value and read a tangible product they can hold in their hands and doesn't force them to go online to access content through their computer or portable device.

Brochures and sales literature: Unlike print media, which goes to an entire subscriber base, brochures and sales literature allow for specific targeting on a direct, one-to-one basis.

Telephone: The phone is another marketing opportunity. Due to rampant misuse in the past, laws now limit how marketers can use the telephone. But it's still a workable marketing channel.

Marketing by telephone, sometimes called telemarketing, exists in two forms. Inbound telemarketing is when people call you. Outbound telemarketing is where you call customers and prospects.

We further divide outbound telemarketing into calling businesses (business-to-business or B2B marketing) and calling consumers (business-to-consumer or B2C marketing). Both face legal restrictions, especially B2C, that marketers must carefully adhere to or face significant fines.

Businesses can handle both inbound and outbound telephone calls in-house, or they can outsource the work to a call center—called a teleservice company—that specializes in telephone communication.

Though businesses can outsource telephone calls to a company in another country, called offshoring, most outsourcing occurs within the same country. This effectively negates cultural differences and language barriers.

Broadcast media: Next comes broadcast media, such as radio and television. Both options have seen significant changes in the last couple of decades, yet they still are a workable marketing tool to place advertising messages that will blanket an entire audience.

Trade shows: Over the years I've been to many trade shows, sometimes as an exhibitor and other times as an attendee. Trade shows provide a wonderful opportunity for in-person networking, as well as to learn more and gain valuable industry insights.

When you go to a trade show—either as an exhibitor or as an attendee—go with a plan and work your plan. Make the most of every minute. Don't skip sessions or leave early. Stay throughout the entire event and linger if there's a chance for meaningful interaction with customers or prospects.

Books: You may be surprised to see books on this list of marketing opportunities. This is the most recent development and has two primary applications.

The first use of books as a means of marketing is for a consultant. They publish a book about their area of expertise to position themselves as a subject-matter expert. The book becomes a marketing vehicle and can serve as a most effective business card when given to a prospect.

The other use of books is by CEOs and other high-profile leaders of corporations and nonprofits. Though this can also be of the subject-matter-expert variety, these books more often take the form of a biography or autobiography. By promoting the CEO or leader, the book subtly—and most effectively—highlights the company or organization.

Other traditional marketing: Many other forms of traditional marketing exist. These include networking, referrals, billboards and signs, spotlights and loudspeakers, door-to-door selling, making cold calls, passing out flyers, and so forth.

When use wrongly, the buying public views these as a nuisance, which creates a negative marketing outcome. Yet when used appropriately and smartly, they can produce positive results.

Online Marketing

A newer form of marketing exists online. In general, the impact of online marketing is easier to measure, with the results quantifiable. As such, online marketing is attractive to many.

Here are some forms of online marketing:

Websites: Having an online presence is essential for any business or organization. The ideal solution is a website. When done correctly, you own and control your website. No one (aside from a totalitarian regime) can limit the number of customers and prospects who visit your website.

Use your website to tell others about your organization and its offerings. In addition to company and product information, a website can have an online store or be an entry point into your sales funnel. From your website, collect email addresses for follow-up and ethical email marketing campaigns.

You can tap other forms of traditional and online marketing to drive traffic to your website.

Content marketing: Content marketing is an indirect form of promotion that gives valuable content to your audience. The goal is producing usable information, not selling. By supplying resources that address the needs of prospects, you indirectly promote your organization as a subject-matter expert. This positively predisposes the people who read your content into later doing business with you.

The best place for content marketing is your own website in the form of a professional blog. You can also arrange to post on other sites or even on social media (though I don't advocate social for this application).

Content marketing also has its place in niche print publications. We'll cover this in more detail in the "Part 4: Marketing Tactics" section.

Social media: Though some advocate using social media for an online presence, doing so is risky. A social media platform limits its users' messaging to the very audience who wants to hear from them. The solution to reach this audience is paid advertising.

While social media has its place, consider it as the spokes of a marketing wheel, with your website being its hub.

Social media advertising: As we mentioned, most social media platforms limit your ability to reach your audience. The solution is to advertise on those platforms. These ads can be in the form of text, graphics, or videos.

Currently, the leading social media advertising platforms are Facebook, Instagram, Twitter, YouTube, TikTok, Pinterest, and LinkedIn. Other options include Reddit, Snapchat, Nextdoor, and Quora.

To find out more about advertising on social media, just search for the platform's name along with the word *advertising*. But don't try to advertise on every platform that offers the option.

Pick the ones where your target audience is, establish a presence there, and understand how the platform works. Then explore advertising on it. Once you've mastered that platform, then consider a second one.

Online advertising: Online advertising exists in two forms.

The most common online marketing option is going to ad platforms, such as running Google ads or Microsoft ads.

The second option is placing custom banner ads on curated websites whose traffic demographics align with your target market. Because this is a one-to-one placement effort, this is a time-consuming consideration, yet for the right site it is most cost-effective.

Email marketing: Sending marketing messages by email can be a cost-effective way to reach your prospects and upsell your customers, providing you do it correctly and legally.

Never buy an email list or scrape contact information from the internet. Aside from existing customers, only contact prospects who want to hear from you and have given their permission for you to contact them through email.

When emailing, don't send the same message to everyone. Segment your list based on their interest level, their status as a customer or prospect, and where they fit in your sales funnel. Make sure every message moves them forward on the customer journey or toward buying from you.

Don't email too often. And do give readers the option to self-select what messages they want to receive and when.

Summary

Consider this list of marketing channels when developing your strategy and designing a well-rounded promotional plan. We'll expand on some of these options in upcoming chapters.

Marketing Management Success Tip

All these promotion opportunities offer a wide array of marketing channels for you to consider in getting the word out about your company and offerings. Select them with care and use them responsibly to achieve the best results.

Tracking Marketing Effectiveness

When Marketing Data Is Absent, You Need to Go by Instinct

T hough the source of the old advertising quip is in dispute, its wisdom isn't. The adage laments, "Half the money I spend on advertising is wasted; the trouble is I don't know which half."

Tracking Traditional Marketing

When it comes to traditional marketing channels, there's so much truth in this saying. As marketers, we never know how many people respond to any given ad or, of those who respond, how many buy. Yes, we can survey new customers and ask, "Where did you hear about us?", but even that collected information is in doubt.

Remember when I said I once ran Yellow Pages ads? This was before the dawn of the World Wide Web and, later, at its early inception, when it was still a novelty. Back then, the Yellow Pages was the go-to source for finding the product or service you needed. As I recall, I advertised in over fifty directories in various markets and from different publishers. But I never knew which ads worked, which were cost effective, or the ROI of any of them.

In an effort to find clarity and obtain actionable data, I had each sales rep ask new clients, "Where did you hear about us?" This was even a question on their onboarding paperwork. If they said, "the Yellow Pages," the follow-up question was "which one?"

To my dismay, 4 percent of those who cited the Yellow Pages named a non-existent directory as the one they consulted. This brought into question the value of any of their feedback.

In addition to worrying about the accuracy of their responses, I questioned if they gave me the best answer. Given the conventional wisdom that it takes at least seven touches to make an impact on a potential buyer before they become a customer, I wondered which one they gave me. Was it the first touch, the final one, the most notable one, or simply the first one that came to mind? I suspect the latter. Or, feeling pressure to respond quickly, they could have even made up an answer.

The only thing worse than no data is bad data.

In the end, I had to go by what my gut told me and what my marketing budget allowed.

True, some ads were so inexpensive that one sale justified them for the entire year. The same applied to some of my print media advertising. Yet when the budget is tight, it's easy to cancel ads that you can't prove are working.

Tracking Online Marketing

This inability to track marketing effectiveness doesn't carry over to the online world. There we have plenty of data, perhaps too much.

For online advertising, we can look at impressions and clicks, which allow us to calculate our clickthrough rate (CTR). If the sale is completed online, we know how many sales the ad produced, allowing us to calculate cost per sale and clicks per sale.

If we really want to get into the weeds, we can track this by day of the week and time of day. We can look at weekend versus weekday and daytime versus night-time, along with seasonal fluctuations. We can also track results by geography and factor in socioeconomic data.

With social media, we can look at reach, followers, and interaction, be it a like, a forward, or a comment—whatever analogous label occurs on a particular platform. And when we pay a social media platform to get our message out, we can track results much like any other online ad.

We also have interesting metrics for email marketing. We can look at delivery rate, open rate (all the while knowing that technology underreports results), and click rate. Looking at the number of replies is useful, as is the number of unsubscribes.

Even content marketing has helpful statistics, such as the number of page views, comments, likes, and shares. Yet connecting these forms of engagement to sales is difficult, making content marketing the least data-rich online marketing option. Still, it's much better than having no information.

The Response

The reaction of some marketers—especially younger ones who grew up with the internet and those with a more recent marketing degree—is to focus on online marketing, where they can measure results and quantify sales. Alternately, they dismiss traditional marketing—which they can't track—with suspicion, knowing that it wastes half of their advertising dollars, if not more. They just don't know which half.

This is understandable, but not the wisest marketing approach. Be sure to consider all marketing options—both traditional and online. This doesn't mean, however, that you should pursue them all. Just contemplate them.

Therefore, employ the marketing options that make sense for your target audience and business strategy, using both traditional and online marketing channels as appropriate. Whenever possible, track what you can to gauge results and drive continued investment. For the rest, accept the unknowable as a part of doing business and embrace the mystery of it, using all the experience you have to produce meaningful insight.

Marketing Management Success Tip

Embrace the reality that marketing is part science and part art.

CHANNEL INCONSISTENCY

Frustration Abounds When Details Differ Between the Store, Online, and Call Center

Every two years my family and I upgrade our cell phones. This isn't because we want the newest model. It's because we seek the lowest cost. Since each provider offers better deals to new customers than existing ones, we're forced to switch carriers.

Every time we make our biennial switch, a nightmare unfolds. Here's one of our tales of frustration.

In Person

This time, our daughter took the lead in our every-other-year phone migration. She replaced her phone first. She did her research online and then visited their store to complete the purchase. The phone she selected had an instant rebate and a mail-in rebate, which resulted in a cost of zero. Everything went as expected, and she bought her new phone.

We thought nothing of the fact that the website promotion matched the in-store price. Assuming this would continue to be true, however, was a mistake.

With her approval of the product, a few weeks later we moved forward to replace three more phones. With confidence we returned to the store, only to learn the price for that phone had increased and there was no longer a mail-in rebate.

We left discouraged and without our new phones.

Online

Once home, we revisited their website. Online pricing had changed too, but it differed from the store's price. The cyberspace deal offered an instant rebate, resulting in a net cost of 99 cents. Though a tad more than free, we accepted the charge. I placed the order, but a pop-up told me I couldn't upgrade online. It referred me to a toll-free number.

Call Center Sales

I called. Incredibly, their net price after rebate was $50, not 99 cents. When I mentioned the online offer, the agent matched it.

A few days later, I phoned them again to order a fifth and final unit. To my dismay, I hadn't noted the 800-number given online in the pop-up window. Instead of repeating a futile pretense of ordering online just to get it, I dialed the number listed on my paperwork.

Call Center Customer Service

This time I encountered yet another pricing situation. The net cost, after promotions and rebate, would be $40 to buy the same phone. I told the agent about the deal I received two days prior. This confused her, musing about the different options she could tap to give me a better deal. She could reduce my cost to $29.95, even $20—with manager approval—but not 99 cents.

I mentioned the website deal and asked her to match it. She told me she couldn't do that.

"But the person I talked to on Monday matched it," I said.

Again, this confused her. After more questioning, she understood the situation. She was in customer service while the prior employee was in sales. Sales could match website offers; customer service could not.

She surprised me by revealing she had a sales quota of two phones per day. Although she remained professional, her enthusiasm waned. She gave me the number for sales, lessening her chances of meeting her daily quota.

I called the number and bought the phone for 99 cents.

Four Prices

To recap, the store promoted one price, the website listed another, customer service offered a third, and sales quoted a fourth. Customer service had some pricing latitude, but sales had more.

Is this any way to run a business?

Subjecting frontline staff to inconsistent pricing and frustrating policies is no way to treat employees. Nor is it the right way to treat customers.

Everyone suffers with channel inconsistency between the physical store, the website, and the call center. This disconnect affects staff, prospects, and customers. The result is buyers venting to staff. Frontline employees—store clerks and call center agents—must endure this understandable, but avoidable, customer angst.

What we must offer is channel consistency.

Marketing Management Success Tip

Channel inconsistency is no longer as bad as it once was. But it still exists. Hire a secret shopper. Have them interact with your company through each channel to uncover inconsistencies in pricing and policies. Then eliminate the differences.

Your customers and your frontline staff will appreciate it.

Your Company's Online Presence

Focus on Your Website Which You Own and Control

Most medium-sized and large companies have a website. And successful organizations have one too. Yet some smaller or older companies struggle in this area. Some don't have a website, while others have one, but it's outdated or substandard.

Here are some tips to help you move forward in setting up a practical online presence you can be proud of.

The Role of Social Media

Some organizations make the mistake of foregoing a website. They try to use social media for their online presence. This is a bad idea. First, they don't own their social media page and can be kicked off it at any time, for any reason. Contrast this to a website, which a company owns and controls.

This doesn't mean to ignore social media, but the goal of social media pages should be to direct people to your website. Think of social media as the spokes of the wheel and your website as the hub.

Website Basics

Although it can cost tens of thousands of dollars to design a professional-looking website, there are less costly options. After all, we don't all drive a luxury car; sometimes entry-level transportation will do just fine.

In truth, you can make an inexpensive website yourself for under $100. The goal is for it to not *look* cheap. Most hosting companies offer do-it-yourself website templates you can customize to provide a basic, yet professional-looking, site. If you want to avoid using predesigned templates, WordPress.org is a popular alternative.

Regardless, there are a few beginner mistakes you will want to avoid:

- Stay away from line art graphics or any artwork that looks homemade.

- If you need to resize a graphic, be sure to keep it proportional. Otherwise, it will distort and look odd.

- Proofread the text, verify spelling, use correct grammar, and employ commonly accepted punctuation.

- Have others double-check your content. Then have someone else triple-check it.

- Don't go crazy with different fonts. Use one or two at the most.

- Have a consistent style and color palette throughout.

- Avoid uppercase text; people will feel like you're screaming at them. (The one possible exception *might* be when listing your company name at the top of the page.)

- Use italics sparingly. It's hard to read in large blocks.

- Don't insert some nifty gadget on your site. Resist the urge. Just because these features are available doesn't mean you should use them.

- Also be wary of animation, videos that play automatically, and sound that's turned on by default. If you irritate a visitor they'll bounce from your site and never return.

Also, don't piggyback off someone else's domain name; get your own. You can inexpensively obtain a domain name from your hosting company. While you're at it, set up an email account using *that* domain name. Post that email address on your website. If necessary, you can have this new address forward to an existing email account.

Search Engine Optimization

Now that you have a functioning website—which avoids all the above beginner errors—you want people to find it. Aside from telling everyone you meet and listing it on every piece of literature and stationery you have, you need search engines to notice and appreciate your website. This is called search engine optimization (SEO).

Since the search engine companies closely guard their methodologies, SEO is more of an art form than an exact science. Even so, here are some common SEO basics:

- Each page needs a title. This will help both visitors and search engines.

- Each page needs a description; don't use the same description on every page or repeat descriptions.

- Add correct keywords. Although most search engines ignore them, some search engines may still look at them. Again, keywords should not be the same for each page.

Although some people still pursue reciprocal linking (that is, "I'll link to your site if you link to mine"), this no longer helps and could hurt your visibility with search engines. Don't do it.

Many of the companies that guarantee you top search engine placement do not deliver or can't sustain it. There are experts who can do this, but they are in a minority and their skill is often hard to verify.

If you hire someone to improve your website's SEO, you have every right to expect results and to hold them accountable.

Content Marketing

If you want people to find your site and contact you, the next step to consider is content marketing. This is when you post helpful, non-salesy information on your website as a no-strings-attached public service. This content should be relevant to your company and helpful to your prospects. In doing so you become a subject-matter expert in the eyes of your audience.

Search engines serve up this content to people who seek it. The result is traffic to your site. After they read what they came there to find, an attractive and helpful website will keep them there. Hopefully, some of them will want to learn more about your company or your products and services.

Ongoing Work

A website isn't a set-it-and-forget-it effort. A website benefits from ongoing tweaking to make it more valuable to your target audience. Also, expectations change over time, as do best practices.

Expect to continue to work on your website on an ongoing basis to fine-tune and improve it.

Outsourcing

You can outsource any or all these steps, but it comes at a cost. As an alternative, you can do it yourself. Regardless of which path you take, don't expect immediate results. It takes time to perfect a website and drive traffic to it.

The best time to make your website was ten years ago. The second-best time is today.

Marketing Management Success Tip

If you don't have a website, you need one. And if you have a website, work to make it better. In either case, the results will increase visibility and leads.

How to Succeed at Email Marketing

Don't Overlook or Dismiss This Proven and Stable Channel

E mail marketing is a cost-effective and straightforward way to reach out to touch prospects. But just because it's cheap and easy doesn't mean it's always the best idea. When done wrong, email marketing can alienate the audience you're trying to cultivate.

Here are five tips for successful email marketing:

Send Only Useful Messages

Several years ago, I had the grand idea of using an email-marketing program to inform and engage advertisers and potential advertisers for my magazines. When I began working on the next issue, I emailed them with the theme and deadlines. A week before the due date, I sent a reminder. When the magazine went to print, I dashed off an update, and when it mailed, I let them know.

This lasted for two issues.

Although sending the messages seemed free, it cost me time. I also worried about becoming a nuisance. And in those early days of email marketing, I couldn't tell who was reading what I sent.

I scaled back my messages to one per issue. That email let them know the theme and deadlines. It's what mattered most. Besides, if I emailed less often, I hoped they'd be more apt to read what I did send.

Only send the messages that matter to your audience.

Segment Your Audience

I quickly fell into a rhythm of sending out one email as I prepared each issue, but it wasn't as smooth as I hoped. It seemed that no matter how carefully I worded my message, someone would be confused. This resulted in more communication to clear up my miscommunication.

The problem was that I tried to make one email work for everyone: regular advertisers, occasional advertisers, and potential advertisers. A message for regular advertisers might confuse the occasional ones and vice versa. Alternately, a message encouraging potential advertisers to run an ad might cause regular advertisers to make wrong assumptions about their status. To solve this, I divided my list into three groups and sent specific messages tailored to each audience.

Your biggest customer is different than your smallest, and both are different from your prospects. Segment your list appropriately.

Send Only Wanted Messages

As a result of inquiring about a product or service, I often end up on a company's email list. I'm okay with them following up with me or sending more information—as long as it's relevant. Just because I inquired about one thing, however, doesn't mean I'm interested in everything they offer.

If they do this once, I'll overlook it. If they do this twice, I'll unsubscribe. Then they lost the ability to connect with me.

Allow Unsubscribes

Even though it's a requirement to let people unsub-scribe, I'm shocked at how many email marketers don't. Plus, a few let you try to unsubscribe, but they don't follow through.

Allow for and honor unsubscribes. It's the right thing to do.

Don't Spam

Though I have no firsthand experience in this regard, it's easy to buy an email database. It's also common for companies to harvest contact information and send you messages you don't want. These messages are spam.

In your zeal to market, make sure you don't spam your list or look like a spammer.

Marketing Management Success Tip

Send useful messages to your segmented list, allow for unsubscribes, and avoid spamming. This will put you ahead of most companies. Then provide the right amount of contact, and your email marketing is poised to succeed.

PROMOTING CHURN

Disrespecting Customers Is the Fastest Way to Lose Them

Though not as frequent as our biennial cell phone migration from one carrier to another, my family and I have all too often found ourselves forced to change entertainment providers due to escalating charges. These companies have the same mentality as the phone carriers. They offer attractive incentives to gain new business and then jack up the rates, forcing customers to seek low-cost alternatives from their competition.

For several years we enjoyed bundled internet and television service from one provider. They offered attractive pricing for both services, which we were happy to pay. Committing to two years with them, they committed to two years of no price increases. After our 24-month contract ended, we continued with them on a month-to-month basis.

Then the price increases began.

Escalating Rates

They first increased their fees on our television package. Every six months or so they raised prices to provide us with the same level of entertainment. Each time my wife would see what she could do to lower our bill. Sometimes this required another commitment and other times we needed to scale back our options. Even then, the net result was often a price increase. And every time she did this required multiple phone calls and too much wasted time.

Though not as aggressive, they also inched up the rate for internet access. Over time they increased our bill 50 percent. Yet, as the only choice for a stable, high-speed connection, we had to accept it.

This wasn't the case with entertainment. We had options. At the point when our television package nearly tripled from the original amount, and even after scaling back the number of channels, my wife had enough. She was ready to switch.

Several companies offered more for less. Our new entertainment provider charged 20 percent less than our *initial* bill from our existing provider. As a bonus, the new provider offered more channels, superior recording options, and better technology.

Their Best Wasn't Good Enough

Before we switched, however, my wife made a final plea to our existing provider. She begged them for their best deal. They refused to budge. She even told them what both they and we knew would happen. "Once we cancel, you'll offer us a great deal to come back. Can't you just give us that deal now?"

"No. You're already getting the best deal we can offer to an existing customer."

She canceled service, and we switched entertainment providers. The side effect was that, without being bundled, our internet access rate went up. Even so, we still saved money. And we loved the service from our new entertainment provider.

The Marketing Onslaught

As expected, our internet service provider began trying to get us to return and buy our entertainment package from them too. Several years later, they're still trying.

They are most aggressive. Each month they mail us at least two promotions to entice us to return. They also include a one-page ad in each invoice. In addition, they send several emails each month.

Though it shouldn't be a surprise, the deal they offer has the same rates we had when we first signed up several years before.

More recently, they've given up offering to bundle internet and entertainment. Now they're offering to bundle internet and cell phones. The email frequency has increased, too. It seems like I get something at least once a week. I now no longer even glance at their messages and just delete them. This means that if they send me a truly important email, I'll never read it.

In addition, each marketing initiative serves as a painful reminder of how poorly they treated me as a customer. Why would I want to buy more services from them and repeat the process?

Marketing Management Success Tip

If customer churn is part of your business, strive to reverse the trend. Empower your staff to keep existing customers instead of trying to win them back once you've chased them away.

A Lesson in Futility

Unethical Business Practices Hurt Everyone

T he deluge of phone calls was not how I wanted to start my week. These calls slammed my company's sales line—with complaints against another company. What unfolded was a revealing look at the ugliness of unethical marketing tactics.

Though I haven't had a fax machine in years, there was a time when most businesses did. This story harkens from that era, yet its lessons remain relevant today and apply to the present use of email, phone calls, and social media. Be sure not to repeat this mistake of yesterday in how you use technology today.

Fine Print

The calls came from irate—and often not-too-polite individuals—thinking they were calling a fax removal line. They had received an unwanted fax solicitation from a travel company offering 75 percent off Florida and Bahamas cruise vacations.

Not impressed, these angry people called the fax removal line listed in the fine print at the bottom of the fax to stop the unwelcome intrusions. The problem was that, between a too-small font and the low reproduction quality of faxes, two fives in the removal phone number looked like two sixes, matching our sales phone number.

With voicemail now screening the calls to our sales line (even a recording saying that callers had *not* reached the fax removal line did not stop them from leaving their information—along with a piece of their angst), I turned my attention toward averting a reoccurrence of this fiasco.

The solution seemed straightforward. Call the number in the ad, ask for a manager, explain the situation, and request that future faxes use a larger point size to display the fax removal number. Boy was I naive.

Boiler Room

I called the phone number in their ad. An agent who cared nothing for professionalism or customer service answered. The cacophony in the background confirmed I'd reached a call center boiler room. Once the agent realized I didn't want to hear her spiel for vacation cruises, she became even less interested in my call. I realized my explanation was futile, so I asked to speak to a supervisor. She hung up on me.

Fuming, I called again, this time reaching a different agent. "Someone just hung up on me," I said and launched into my story.

This rep cut me off. "I'll have your fax number removed from our list," she said with irritation. I tried anew to explain. She responded with the same words, only louder.

"No, you don't understand," I pleaded.

"Yes, I do understand," she yelled back.

I demanded to speak with a manager. I waited on hold for several minutes. After a long delay, a dial tone greeted me.

Hiding

By now, I was furious. I searched online for a different means of contact. Their company name revealed three matches: a forum post complaining about the company, a listing that gave a street address, and a website covering fraud and scams, with the contributor mentioning timeshares and "bait and switch."

The street address gave me two matches in California. I switched to the satellite view, which showed both addresses in residential areas. That didn't help.

I searched online for their phone number. This brought up the prior post about fraud and a number look-up service. These people did not want me to find them.

Any ethical business would have a website and list contact options. But when a sales and marketing outfit works under the covert darkness of anonymity, it's reasonable to assume they have something to hide.

I suspected a service bureau had sent the fax. This same scenario had occurred before. That ad was for a different company, and they did not use a call center.

This time I gave up on the deadbeat marketing company, turning my attention to the fax service bureau that was complicit in the mess. I called the real fax-removal number. I reached a recording, with no way to talk to a person or leave a message. I pressed zero—many times. It tried to remove phone number 000-000-0000. It was already "removed."

Next, I searched online using the fax removal number and got no matches. The faxing service company, it seems, didn't want me to call them either.

Lessons Learned

Even now, I shake my head with disbelief. These types of unrestrained activities and fly-by-night antics by an unscrupulous few have caused problems in the past—and they continue to do so now. This madness must end.

At the risk of stating the obvious, here are some recommendations that apply to all businesses:

- Train staff to be polite and professional. Retrain or terminate those who won't conform.

- Don't hang up on callers.

- Transfer calls to a supervisor or manager whenever asked.

- Make it easy for people to find and contact you. This means having a website and listing your phone number, along with other contact methods.

- Don't use bait and switch tactics.

- Police your staff so they don't take shortcuts or treat customers badly when it doesn't serve their interests.

- Compensate your staff for the results you want. If you only pay for closed sales, expect nothing else from them.

- Don't *force* customers to use automated solutions.

- Provide a way out of automation. Let them press zero for an operator or at least leave a message.

- Offer an alternative means of contact, such as email or even snail mail.

- Don't send illegal or unethical faxes, emails, or chat messages. Don't make illegal phone calls.

- If you perform services for other companies, don't work with unscrupulous clients.

Since you're reading this book, you don't need this advice. But others do. I hope these words will somehow find their way into the hands of a manager or business owner who needs to reform their sales and marketing practices and do right for their customers and prospects.

Marketing Management Success Tip

Confirm that your marketing practices are legal and ethical. Then review your staff's training. Work to make sure they represent your company with excellence, every time.

A Marketing Failure

Use Customer Communications to Strengthen the Business Relationship, Not Ruin It

B ack in the days when I had a physical phone line, my provider changed names. I'm still not sure if this was the result of new ownership or merely a rebranding effort. Regardless, there was much hype surrounding this news, arriving in the form of frequent mailed communications and email messages that spanned several months.

Throughout all this, the phone company repeatedly promised that there would be no rate increases—all that would change was their name. These marketing messages also made hazy hints of new services but withheld helpful details.

My first sign that something was amiss came with my first bill under the new company name. Contrary to their repeated promises, their charges went up, almost doubling. When I called to complain, evoking their pledge, the rep informed me that my past bills had been incorrect. Therefore, they were not bound by their no-increase promise but had the legal requirement to correct the errors. At least the increase was not retroactive.

This should have been sufficient warning to be wary of what they said, but I was slow to master that lesson. When they called me a few months later—a different marketing tactic—to "lower my monthly rate," I was quite excited. With this new plan, I could recover much of what I had lost when they had "corrected" my bill. The rep's mastery of English was questionable, so at each step I repeated back to her everything I understood her to say.

"You're going to lower my monthly base rate for local service to $17.95," I concluded.

"Yes!" she confirmed and then transferred me for third party verification.

Excited, I listened to a recap of my order. "You're signing up for our unlimited long distance calling package at $17.95 a month; this requires—"

"No," I interrupted. "That's not what I want at all." Fortunately, the verification rep's communication was clear and effective, saving me from buying something I didn't want.

So began an all-too-frequent barrage of solicitation calls from my *new* local phone company. Realizing that I couldn't rely on what they told me, I'd end each interruption as fast as possible and return to work. When my irritation over their incessant interruptions became intolerable, I begged them to stop calling me. This proved unsuccessful, so I resorted to hanging up on them. That didn't stop the calls, but it gave me a small degree of vindication.

When their most recent incursion breached my normally idyllic workspace, I listened to their spiel with a more critical ear. To recap: they called a business line about residential service, they didn't know my name, and they had no access to what services I used. At that point, I doubted the call was even from my phone company. Perhaps they had outsourced calling to a shoddy telemarketing firm instead of a reputable one. Or was the call a scam?

When a poorly executed telemarketing effort is indistinguishable from a scam, something is terribly wrong. Intervention is needed.

Marketing Management Success Tip

When pursuing a telemarketing strategy, whether in-house or outsourced, make sure the firm represents your company well and respects your customers and prospects.

PART 4

Marketing Tactics

O ver the years I've done much in the way of content marketing, both for my periodicals and for my books. I also once focused for a time on writing content marketing pieces for others. They appreciated my work and the results, but I no longer have the time to provide this service. Since 2008 I've produced about 5,000 content marketing pieces for myself and others. Each one continues to do its job, supplying valuable information to interested parties and driving web traffic.

Another recent marketing pursuit of mine is internet advertising. I use this to promote my books. This includes Amazon, BookBub, Goodreads, Facebook, Google, and Microsoft. Some produce a significant ROI, others have a much smaller return, and a few have a learning curve that I'm still climbing.

I've also done print media marketing, email marketing, and social media marketing, as well as dabbling in a few others.

Regardless of your industry and promotional focus, remember that any marketing strategy can be a success and any marketing initiative can fail. It depends on the attitude of the person implementing it, the management support they receive, and the staff who do the work.

Pricing, Sales, and Discounts

Price Matters, but Not in the Way You Think

A common complaint I've heard over the years from my sales teams is that the prices for our products or services is too high. Yet in lowering rates to match the competition, it becomes a race to the bottom.

I've seen this taken to an extreme in the book publishing industry where some authors give their books away for free to increase their "sales" numbers or attract readers to buy their other books. Yet it's hard to make a profit when you give away your merchandise.

Price

My response to staff when they complain about prices is to point out that they're focused on the wrong thing. "Never sell by price," I say. "When you gain a client by price, you're going to lose them for the same reason." They'll bail when a lower-cost option comes their way—and it will.

Instead of price, focus on value, benefits, and outcomes. This is hard to do, however, when the first words out of most prospects' mouths are "How much does it cost?"

Yes, sometimes an up-front discussion of cost is needed because it weeds out those with a significant misalignment between what you're selling and what they can afford. There's no use extolling the features of a $10,000 solution when the inquiring buyer has a $250 budget.

Regardless, it's essential to train sales staff to move away from selling by price and instead promote your product or service's virtues.

Though some will surely disagree, as far as I'm concerned, lowering price is not a workable tactic for long-term success or ongoing viability.

Price your product or service appropriately and promote it accordingly.

Sales

Throughout my career I've seldom run sales. From a philosophical standpoint, it's unfair to charge some buyers full price and give others a break.

From a practical standpoint, if you run too many sales too often, you train your customers to never buy at list price and to always wait for a sale. And once you program them to think of you in those terms, it's hard to reprogram them to embrace a full-price mentality.

One office supply company so successfully tempted me to buy with their frequent sales that I stockpiled enough office supplies to cover me for the rest of my life with most items. Yet, their frequent sales promotions so irritated me that I eventually unsubscribed from their email list. Losing my connection with them, I seldom thought of them anymore. In effect, their overzealous sales turned me from a card-carrying member of their loyalty program to someone who hasn't bought from them in a decade.

In expressing my dislike of running sales, I must acknowledge that most of my marketing experience comes from selling products or services with a recurring element. Telephone answering service is billed monthly and periodical advertising reoccurs each issue. For consulting, my strategy was ongoing work from each client. Even with book sales, my goal isn't for a one-off sale but to attract readers who will buy multiple books from me over the years.

When it comes to a business model based on recurring revenue, gaining business through a sale means you perpetuate that special price month after month, year after year. Notably, I don't have experience in selling a manufactured product or in retail sales.

If I did, perhaps I wouldn't have such an aversion to running sales, but I do.

Discounts

A discount is similar to a sale. I've run discounts on occasion. But it's always for a strategic purpose.

For example, when rebranding and changing the operational model of one of my publications, I needed to quickly achieve a buy-in from enough advertisers to create a financial base from which the publication could function. I needed this to cover my overhead costs, and I needed it quickly.

To achieve this goal, I identified my top five prospects and offered them a 50 percent lifetime discount if they would commit prior to the relaunch. I sold all five, and four are still with me years later. Based on their early commitment to my vision, I was able to relaunch the publication and form a stable, workable promotional resource that has produced a profit ever since.

Yes, there are times when I wish I could charge these four charter advertisers full price, but it's worked for them and for me. And I'm content with that.

Marketing Tactics Success Tip

Carefully consider how pricing fits into your marketing strategy. Decide the role running sales will play, if any. Also determine if you will ever offer any discounts and under what conditions.

Approach each consideration from a long-term perspective and not a short-term gain.

RESPECT YOUR EXISTING BUSINESS RELATIONSHIP STATUS

Unrestrained Marketing Can Drive Business Away

I n most cases, businesses face legal restrictions when it comes to calling residential phone numbers. Aside from some carved-out exemptions, the one key exception is if there is an existing business relationship (EBR) between the company and the person they're calling.

So, if you're only making EBR calls, you may think you have nothing to worry about, right? Not so fast. Just because it's legal to dial that number doesn't mean you should.

Simply put, calling too often or for the wrong reasons could turn an EBR into a former EBR. This happened when I retaliated against a company that was overcalling me—and others could do it to you.

I used to have a subscription to the local paper. Since I only had time to read it on the weekends, those were the only days I received it. This was an ideal arrangement, one which I would have gladly continued if not for overzealous telemarketing.

One evening, during dinner, I received a call from an enthusiastic employee of the paper. They had a special upgrade price so that I could enjoy the paper all week long. When would I like to start? I explained that I only wanted the paper on the weekends. Receiving it when I didn't have time to read it would only serve to make me feel guilty—either for wasting time by reading it or for wasting money by not reading it. The agent laughed and said she understood.

A few months later, I received another call with the same offer from a different rep. I assumed turnover had occurred and no one recorded my preference for weekend-only delivery. (So much for an effective customer relationship management system—CRM). I repeated my explanation and again stated my desire for weekend-only delivery.

These calls became a regular occurrence, and I grew increasingly annoyed. Sometimes the interval was two or three months, other times only a couple of weeks, and once it was two days. They always came at an inopportune time.

No one seemed to realize that no matter how often they offered it, I wasn't going to upgrade my subscription. Even when they offered it at no added cost, I declined, citing my concern over landfills.

I even asked them to stop calling, but they ignored me.

My frustration with their continued phone calls grew to where it exceeded my satisfaction from reading their paper. I realized that by canceling my subscription, the EBR provision would soon cease to be a factor, and I would have legal recourse should they continue to harass me.

I expected that the ploy to cancel my subscription would give me one final opportunity to stop the phone calls—and continue receiving the paper, without telemarketing. I was wrong.

Incredibly, when I called to cancel my subscription, no one asked why or gave me a chance to explain that their incessant calls irritated me. Most surprising of all—especially given their proclivity for phoning me—no one made a follow-up call, even though there was a window of opportunity for them to phone and win me back. They never tried.

But the unwelcomed calls stopped.

I do miss the paper—at least a bit. Though I've switched to other national and regional news sources, I'm out of the loop on local happenings. But it's a small price to pay to avoid the incessant dinnertime interruptions to sell me something I've repeatedly declined.

The paper thought they were safe by placing calls that met all legal requirements, but they were wrong. Their unbridled calling turned a happy reader into an irritated former reader.

I wonder how many other subscriptions they lost because of their legal, but unrestrained, calling practices?

Marketing Tactics Success Tip

When it comes to contacting customers, just because you can, doesn't mean you should.

ALIGN MARKETING TACTICS WITH SALES SKILLS

When the Execution of Your Plan Falls Short, It Might Be Time for a New Plan

I n the book-publishing community, it's no secret that most authors would rather write than promote their work. In this regard, I am like most authors. Yes, some writers are extroverts and love the activities around launching and promoting a book. Most, however, are introverts like me.

Add to this the sage advice to "Do what only you can do, and have others do the rest."

That's why I chose to outsource the sales and marketing of my books. At various times over the years, I've hired a book promotion specialist, a book launch team manager, an online ad agency, a book marketing assistant, a social media manager, and an SEO expert.

None produced a positive return on investment, and many produced no return at all. Yet during this time I shelled out tens of thousands of dollars and sold few books for my investment.

That's when I realized I had two choices: don't do any book promotion or do it myself. Reluctantly, I decided to do it myself, all the while knowing this would detract from my writing schedule and reduce my output.

I looked at the conventional book promotion strategies of traditional book publishers, all the while suspecting that much of it no longer applied in today's rapidly changing publishing landscape. I made a list. I also added what leading indie-published authors were doing. Some of the items seem doable and others turned my stomach; just thinking about them made me nauseous.

I divided the items into three categories: yes, maybe, and no. This resulted in a list of marketing I was open to do, a second list of activities I was willing to do if needed, and a final list of tasks I was unwilling to do, the nonnegotiables.

With clarity in place, I set about developing a book marketing strategy that would tap into my "yes list" and avoid my "no list." I'm currently implementing my new marketing plan, and it's producing results.

Consider the lessons we can learn from my development of a marketing plan tailored to my personality, ability, and willingness.

Imagine you're a sales and marketing manager whose strategy hinges on your sales staff making cold calls to move prospects into the sales funnel. Unfortunately, your team struggles making cold calls and resists doing so, even to the point of engaging in passive-aggressive behavior. Repeated efforts to give them needed training and supportive encouragement have failed. And your threats have gone unheeded.

You have two alternatives. One consideration is to replace your sales team with employees willing to engage in cold calls. The other possibility is to look at your existing team's strengths and weaknesses to develop a strategy around them. (Maintaining the status quo isn't an acceptable solution.)

Though a fire-them-all-and-start-over approach may tempt you, I encourage a more enlightened solution of keeping them employed and working with them to tailor a more conducive sales and marketing strategy. This path is even more important if you struggle to find qualified employees in the first place.

Though I doubt your issue is over making cold calls (does anyone do that anymore?), look for a disconnect between your marketing strategy and your team's adherence.

If you can correct this misalignment through retraining them or changing your management style, great. Otherwise, evaluate your team's strengths and weaknesses to develop a fresh sales and marketing plan, one tailored to what they do best and avoids what they struggle with or do poorly.

I did this for my book sales, and you can do it for your team too.

Marketing Tactics Success Tip

If your employees struggle to implement your marketing strategy, it might be time to develop a fresh approach.

A Primer on Ads

Don't Overlook the Basics for Your Marketing Initiatives

As a periodical publisher, I've run ads for my customers. As a marketer, I've created and run ads for myself in various publications and on websites. And as a buyer, I've reacted to ads. These experiences provide me with a 360-degree view, able to see ads from a provider, seller, and buyer perspective.

Whether it's print ads or online, there are two challenges. The first is finding the right publication or platform that addresses your target audience. The second is designing an effective ad.

The Right Medium

When considering a publication or online platform to promote your message, consider their target audience. This is the foremost concern. Even when secondary issues align, if you're talking to the wrong audience, your message will fail to resonate with them and generate the outcome you seek.

Quite simply, do the people you want to reach read the publication or visit the website you're considering? If not, don't pursue it, no matter how attractive the rates or reach.

Only after you find a provider that can successfully reach your target audience should you consider the cost of the ad, the number of people who will see your message, and if it reaches true decision makers.

The Right Ad

Once you've found the perfect advertising medium, you need to design your ad. Some providers will offer to produce an ad for you at no cost, but resist taking them up on their tempting offer. Though they may know how to create ads, they may not know your industry or your business. They may be experts in what they do, but they're not experts in what you do.

If you don't have the skills yourself or in-house support to design a professional ad, outsource the task to a third party who can work with you to produce a compelling message.

This is one time when you shouldn't go with "good enough" or "let's throw this up and see what happens." Strive to get your ad exactly right. This includes the ad copy and the artwork.

Use white space in your ad to your advantage, applying it to call attention to your essential message. Avoid having too much text, which makes your ad hard to read and drives readers away.

Also, be sure to give contact information and include a call to action.

If you fail to produce a compelling ad, your ad will fail to produce the results you seek. At this point, the cost of the ad or its reach doesn't matter.

Ad Outcomes

If your ad doesn't produce the results you want, either you've picked the wrong medium or run the wrong ad. Herein is the painful reality of advertising: the right advertising makes things happen; wrong advertising does nothing—except cost you money.

Marketing Tactics Success Tip

Successful advertising relies on two elements: the ideal medium and the perfect ad. If either area is lacking, so too will your results.

Pursue Content Marketing

Indirectly Promote Your Company and Products by Providing Valuable Industry Information

We've already mentioned content marketing in "Part 3: Marketing Management." Now we'll delve into it more fully as a practical marketing tactic. Having written nearly five thousand content marketing pieces over the past couple of decades, it's a subject I know quite well.

The goal of content marketing isn't like a typical marketing strategy. It's more subtle than that, much more. Its intent isn't to sell. Instead, the goal of content marketing is to establish you or your company as an expert in your industry, a thought leader.

The hoped-for side effect is moving readers into your sales funnel once they know you and trust you as a knowledgeable resource. Be aware, however, that most people who read your content will never buy from you.

Repeat readers, though, are likely to form a high opinion of you for your expertise. They may even recommend you to others who will buy from you, even if they don't.

A content marketing piece should give helpful information as a no-strings-attached public service. It should have no obvious marketing content and must avoid even the hint of a sales pitch. Make sure the content is relevant to your company and helpful to your prospects. This portrays you as a subject-matter expert from the perspective of your target audience.

Content Marketing on Your Website

You can publish content marketing on your own website in the form of a blog. Over time, this takes a huge step forward to gain search engine attention. This is part of search engine optimization—SEO. The result is driving traffic to your site. Be aware, however, that this is not an overnight solution, but a long-term strategy that takes time to pay off.

Even so, a post can go viral and produce an instant impact. And a singular post could also attract the right person who's eager to buy. Though these are both immediate outcomes that could occur, it's unwise to plan on them.

Before you begin a content marketing strategy for your website, dig deep to make sure you have enough to say and are committed to pursuing it over time. Figure out a publishing schedule that is both doable and sustainable. Then stick with it. This may be once a month, once a week, or even multiple times a week.

At one point, I posted fresh content three times a week on my main website. It now has two thousand posts, enjoys solid traffic, and experiences year-over-year growth. Be aware that I wrote my first post in 2008 and have been publishing weekly content ever since. But don't let this discourage you. You can enjoy meaningful results with far less content and time.

Content Marketing on Other Channels

You need not restrict content marketing efforts to your own website. You can also guest post on other sites relevant to your industry. Target sites with more traffic or higher influence than yours.

Assuming they accept guest posts or contributed content, you'll need to pitch your idea to them. If they like your concept, then you write and send them your piece. Alternately, they may skip the pitch step and simply have you submit your completed work.

Before you send it, make sure it's your best writing. Don't send a draft for their feedback or expect them to edit it for you; you should do that before you send it.

A special application that falls under the content marketing umbrella is submitting byline articles to industry periodicals. As a media company, your articles on their site will enjoy greater respect and expanded reach. And if they have a print version of their publication, your content will have the greatest impact and you'll receive even more industry esteem.

Regardless of where your piece is published, one post or article can have a significant impact. This is because they already have traffic and an audience, which is unlike your own website where you need ongoing posts to attract visitors.

The Outcome

Regardless of where it's placed, content marketing is a simple and effective marketing tactic that can provide ongoing, enduring results. It establishes the reputation of you and your company, as well as supplying a subtle, but ongoing, source for leads.

Marketing Tactics Success Tip

Embrace content marketing as part of your overall marketing strategy. It will have a long-term and far-reaching impact that will be hard to match with any other tactic.

SUCCESSFULLY SUBMIT PRESS RELEASES AND INFORMATIVE ARTICLES

Adhere to Best Practices, Follow Guidelines, and Write for Your Audience

Consider this: *"ABC Company, a strategic provider of advanced business technology applications to facilitate organizational utilization of game-changing convergent networks, announced today the release of its unprecedented Widgetizer solution, which is guaranteed to revolutionize existing technological infrastructures overnight."*

This is a fictitious example of an all-too-common press release. On any given business day, I receive multiple news announcements and an article or two. Only a small percentage ever make it into print or get posted online.

Although the practical restriction of limited space in a printed medium is one reason, the reality is that most submissions were doomed from the start—much like the above example of verbosity.

Whether submitting a press release or trying to place an article, when you seek publicity, understanding how publishing works is the first step toward successful placement.

Target Your Submissions

Submitting content to a periodical is not like shooting a shotgun, where pellets disperse in a general area with the hope of some hitting the target. Rather, getting published is more like firing a rifle, where a single, carefully aimed bullet has a good chance for success. True, not every shot will hit, but the chances are much greater than just blasting off a shotgun in all directions.

With email, the temptation is to fire off hundreds of messages at every possible target, regardless of how relevant. Doing so, however, reduces your thoughtfully composed prose to spam, earning it a quick end and damaging your reputation as an email marketer.

A carefully targeted approach is a better way to go.

Know Your Target

My first article submission was published. This gave me a false sense of success. I assumed getting published was easy. The reality was that I knew the target publication. I'd been a subscriber for years. I faithfully read each issue and understood the content and style of the articles they used.

Tap Online Resources

Most periodicals have websites, which often post useful information for aspiring contributors. The first step is to check their website for direction. My publications' websites, for example, give guidelines for writing and submitting articles and press releases, including the preferred length, the method of submission, writing style, and so forth.

Limit Communication

In today's publishing world, some editors will respond to emails about submissions, but most do not. Contacting them when you shouldn't will just irritate them. Only reach out when needed and according to their online submission guidelines.

At best, hope for a brief response. Today's editorial staff must do more, in less time, and with fewer resources. Don't take it personally if they ignore your email or send a terse reply. Make the best of any communication and move forward.

Know Your Subject

My first article was "All About Pagers." I knew the topic well, working for a paging company and with several years of experience. You'd think my writing would have flowed easily. It did not.

As I began to write, I realized how much I didn't know. Fortunately, I was able to find the missing pieces and fill in the gaps. The result was an informative submission that clicked with the editors.

It's easy to spot—and dismiss—authors who write about things they don't understand. Don't be one of them.

Follow Directions

The quickest way for your press release or article to be ignored is to assume the rules don't apply to you. Editors more readily use material that follows their guidelines and needs less editing. They don't make rules just because they can, but to make the process easier for everyone.

If they request your submissions via an email attachment (my preferred method), then do it. Other publications avoid attachments and prefer the text be in the body of the email.

Also, if a piece is too long, the publication will edit it for length. The reality is, when an editor is on deadline or pushed for time, content requiring significant editing will often be delayed or deleted.

Increase your chances of publication by simply following directions.

Don't Miss Deadlines

Deadlines exist for a reason. Without them, a publication would never make it to the printer. Be aware and follow submission deadlines (usually posted online and printed in each issue).

If you promise an article by a certain date, don't miss it. If you want your hot news item to be in a specific issue, get it in on time; sooner is better. Weekly papers—and especially magazines—have a much longer lead-time than most people imagine, so be aware of it and adhere to it.

Third Person Preferred

Writing objectively in the third person gives your piece integrity. It's more credible. First person is never acceptable in news releases as it comes across as self-serving, bragging, or unnecessarily introspective.

Always write press releases as an impartial third party. Articles generally work best in this same style. Notable exceptions are how-to pieces and first-hand accounts—such as this book. If you have any doubt about which style to use, act like a reporter and write in third person.

Proofread Carefully

Too often, I receive press releases and articles that have serious errors. Some writers didn't even bother to spell-check their work. This is a sure way to lose credibility and frustrate an editor. Make their work easier by double-checking yours.

Enlist the help of a coworker or hire your own editor. It's not realistic to successfully proof your own work. This is because you know what you intended to write, so that's how you read it, easily overlooking errors and mistakes.

Expect Edits

It's tough to work hard on a piece only to have someone else change it. Similarly, it's easy to become enamored with what you wrote, wanting to see it published verbatim. But this is unrealistic.

Even the most experienced authors have their work edited. This can be for many reasons. A common one is length, another is style, and a third is content suitability. Sometimes giving a piece a different slant makes it better fit a publication's focus. Or an editor may remove a section because it doesn't work well with the issue.

Although some publications have a reputation for twisting, manipulating, or even corrupting an author's work, most make a good-faith effort to retain the writer's intent and present their work in a positive way.

Avoid Hyperbole

The more spectacular the language, the less believable it is. Overused words include "unique," "revolutionary," "leading," and "premier." Avoid them in your writing. Exaggerated copy and unsubstantiated claims only serve to push away readers and weary editors. Yes, clever wording has its place, but when it surpasses the message, something is wrong, and clear communication doesn't occur.

Conclusion

There's no guaranteed way to get your news item or article published, but implementing these ideas will increase the chance of that happening.

Marketing Tactics Success Tip

The more effort you put into crafting a professional and engaging piece for a publication or website, the greater the likelihood of having it published.

THE IDEAL FOLLOW-UP STRATEGY

Strive to Help Each Prospect

O nce I researched some software that promised to streamline my publishing business and integrate operations, as well as provide me with new tools. Given all this, I suspected it would be pricey. But why not dream a little? It wouldn't hurt to get prices. I might even be surprised.

Using an online resource guide that compared the key factors of the major players' offerings, I narrowed the list down to four promising contenders. I sent each one an email, asking the entry-level price and sharing my contact information.

I requested pricing for two reasons. First, if the cost was astronomical, I could opt out of further interaction and not waste any more of my time or theirs. I also hoped to begin a dialogue, allowing me to learn more about the product and company.

Minimal or No Follow-Up

Of the four, one responded right away, two the next day, and one never did. All three responses had a terse statement of price. Only one asked a follow-up question. Another promised to send me a demo, but never did. For the third, I needed clarification on his poorly worded message, which garnered me another brusque email.

Although my first communication was via email, I gave my phone number and mailing address. Sadly, after that initial week, no one bothered to email, call, or mail. They never added me to their marketing databases for future communication.

Of the three prices, one was too high. The second price was also shocking, but acceptable if the software worked as promised. The third, although also high, wasn't unrealistic. If either of these latter two software packages lived up to their grand promises, I'd have bought them, likely within the month. But we'll never know because no one bothered to follow up.

I'm perplexed. At the price of a decent used car, you'd think there would be enough motivation to pursue all leads.

Mindless Follow-Up

The opposite of no follow-up is pointless follow-up. It's even more troublesome because each purposeless contact serves as an effective reminder to *not* buy from that company.

Take Joe for instance. He was a good-ole-boy salesman, with an order-taker mentality. He stumbled onto my name and called for an appointment. Though I said I wanted to interact over the telephone and through email, he pressed for an in-person meeting. Since I had some interest in what he was peddling—and based on his assurances of top-notch customer service and competitive pricing—I eventually agreed to meet.

During our appointment, it became clear that his company wasn't a good match for me. If Joe's demeanor was common, customer service would also be lacking. He confirmed my conclusion of a mismatch with a quote at twenty-five percent higher than competitive prices. I told him so and concluded by saying I'd call him if I wanted to pursue things further.

Sadly, Joe didn't hear me, but my name and number were now in his contact list. Mechanically, he periodically called, not for any real purpose, but just to talk. He never supplied more information, shared company news, or tried to move the sales process forward. His spiel was always along the lines of, "Hi, this is Joe. I'm just checkin' in to see how you're doin'."

At first, I was cordial and would conclude each call with, "I'll call you if I need something." Over time I became less affable, eventually saying, "Joe, please don't call me anymore. I will call you if I need something." Although necessary, I felt horrible for being so blunt.

My dismay was short-lived, because two weeks later, he called again. I cut him off, and said, as politely as I could, "Joe, I don't wish to be rude, but I asked you not to call me anymore. Please don't call again."

This may have been the first time he actually listened. "D-d-did I do something to offend you?" he stammered. I explained my perspective. Incredibly, he called again a few weeks later, spewing his tired old rhetoric. That was the last I heard from him. Either he finally got the message, or he was rightly fired.

Follow Up Until They Decide

You may think me a malcontent, first complaining about a lack of follow-through and then being critical over too much. However, there's a middle ground that salespeople should aim for.

Quite simply, follow up until you hear a yes or a no. And never assume the lead isn't a good lead or presume the prospect will say "no"; wait until they actually say it.

If they're not ready to make a yes or no decision, you should continue doing your job until they decide.

However, even when a prospect says "no," they may not mean "never." Ask if they might want to revisit the situation in the future. If so, make sure you contact them at that time but not before.

Use Care in How Often You Follow Up

Many salespeople ask, "When shall I check back with you?" This seems a wise tactic, but the uninterested, passive-aggressive prospect will simply opt for a time as far in the future as possible, without the need to say no. All that does is string the salesperson along and waste time. Better is to ask what other information the prospect needs from you or what the next step is in their decision-making process.

Have a Reason for Each Contact

Don't call just to chat. Contact them only when you have a purpose or sales-related goal, such as to supply more information, share about new products or services, or offer a special promotion.

When you follow this middle ground, your interactions will have more value and your communication will be better received. Then you'll be more likely to make a sale and less apt to read about your failure in a book.

Marketing Tactics Success Tip

Listen to your prospects, have a purpose with each interaction, and follow up until they decide.

MOVING FORWARD

You Can Do It

As we mentioned in the introduction, everyone has a sales and marketing aspect to both their job and their personal life, even if they don't know it.

Yet some pursue sales and marketing as a career, a calling even. Whether your focus is on management or implementation, whether you address sales or marketing, or maybe you touch on all aspects, this book has suggested ideas to help you move forward.

Review the success tips at the end of each chapter. Enter each one that resonates with you in a planner or journal. This forms the basis for your action plan. Now pick the top three, with an eye toward feasibility and potential results.

Use your top three success tips to set tangible goals for the rest of this year. Pick one as your primary focus, using the second and third to round out your sales and marketing success initiatives. Commit to pursuing and achieving them in the months ahead.

But don't wait for January 1 to roll around. Start today.

Note where you are now and chart your progress month by month. With a commitment to making incremental improvements, you will end the year in a much better place than where you started, realizing greater sales and marketing success.

Repeat this process each year, picking three new success tips to guide your path forward.

A career in sales and marketing isn't easy. If it was, anyone could do it. A career in sales and marketing is hard, which makes the rewards for success even sweeter as you produce positive long-term results and relationships.

May you move forward with confident expectation of achieving greater outcomes than ever before.

You can do it!

OTHER BOOKS IN THE STICKY SERIES

Sticky Customer Service: Stop Churning Customers and Start Growing Your Business

Sticky Leadership: Lead Well to Produce Business Success and Inspire Loyalty (coming 2023)

Sticky Living: Live a Life that Matters to Your Family, Friends, and Community (coming 2024)

About Peter Lyle DeHaan

P eter Lyle DeHaan, PhD, is an entrepreneur and businessman who has managed, owned, or started multiple businesses over his career, with a focus on call centers and then publishing. Common themes at every turn have included sales and marketing, customer service, and leadership and management. He now shares his lifetime of business experience and personal insights with others through his books and blogs to encourage, inspire, and occasionally entertain.

Learn more and see all his books at peterlyledehaan .com.